AMPED UP

Aly & AJ

by Grace Norwich

PSS!
PRICE STERN SLOAN

GROSSET & DUNLAP
Published by the Penguin Group
Penguin Group (USA) Inc., 375 Hudson Street, New York, New York 10014, USA
Penguin Group (Canada), 90 Eglinton Avenue East, Suite 700, Toronto, Ontario M4P 2Y3,
Canada
(a division of Pearson Penguin Canada Inc.)
Penguin Books Ltd., 80 Strand, London WC2R 0RL, England
Penguin Group Ireland, 25 St. Stephen's Green, Dublin 2, Ireland
(a division of Penguin Books Ltd.)
Penguin Group (Australia), 250 Camberwell Road, Camberwell, Victoria 3124, Australia
(a division of Pearson Australia Group Pty. Ltd.)
Penguin Books India Pvt. Ltd., 11 Community Centre, Panchsheel Park, New Delhi—110 017,
India
Penguin Group (NZ), 67 Apollo Drive, Rosedale, North Shore 0632, New Zealand
(a division of Pearson New Zealand Ltd.)
Penguin Books (South Africa) (Pty.) Ltd., 24 Sturdee Avenue,
Rosebank, Johannesburg 2196, South Africa

Penguin Books Ltd., Registered Offices: 80 Strand, London WC2R 0RL, England

Photo Credits: Cover: courtesy of Sheryl Nields/montageagency; Insert photos: pages 1–11
courtesy of Carrie Michalka; pages 12–13 courtesy of Michael Williams/Startracks Photo;
pages 14–15 courtesy of Carrie Michalka; page 16 courtesy of Joe Magnani; Interior photos:
124–125 courtesy of Joe Magnani.

Library of Congress Cataloging-in-Publication Data is available.

ISBN 978-0-448-44841-1   10 9 8 7 6 5 4 3 2 1

TABLE OF

CONTENTS

1   The Nation's First Sisters.....................................5

2   Twins, Two Years Apart..11

3   Little Sister Leads the Way...................................22

4   Aly Steps into the Spotlight.................................33

5   Walking on Sunshine...46

6   A Huge Rush in Sales..59

7   Move Over, Lindsay and Hilary..........................70

8   Keepin' the Faith..81

9   Sisters For Life...91

10   Extraordinary Girls, Regular Lives....................96

11   What's Next?...108

12   Sister Style Guide...111

13   Discography..119

14   Fun Fast Facts..123

15   Web Sightings...127

CHAPTER ONE:
The Nation's First Sisters

It's Easter Sunday 2006. On the South Lawn of the White House in Washington, D.C., scores of happy kids take part in the annual Easter Egg Roll. They're all decked out in their Sunday finest as they play all sorts of games with the little pastel-colored eggs. If not for the Secret Service men in dark suits and sunglasses manning the perimeter, the scene could be happening in any backyard in any neighborhood in America.

On a balcony overlooking the Egg Roll, a small stage has been set up. The crew is running one final check on the microphones and speakers. Everything has to be perfect. This is the White House, after all. Not only that, but the song that's just moments away from being performed is "The Star Spangled Banner."

The words *one, two, one, two* echo crisply over the

manicured lawn. But if the egg rollers notice the sound check, they're not letting on. Their indifference won't last for long, however, because the White House event planners haven't chosen just anyone to belt out this year's Easter Sunday national anthem. Instead, they've settled on the hottest siblings since Jessica and Ashlee Simpson. The toast of the afternoon will be none other than Aly and AJ Michalka!

Backstage, the newly anointed princesses of pop must have been feeling the pressure. Sure, by the spring of 2006, they were used to performing in front of legions of crazed fans. But the president of the United States? "That was amazing," Aly says. "AJ and I just freaked out. We were so nervous before that because, of course, it's the president. We were, like, 'Oh gosh we have to be right on top of it.'"

Fortunately, wowing crowds is what Aly and AJ do best. In a world of one-hit wonders, the sisters from Southern California are the real deal. Drawing on the influence of such bona fide rockers as Heart, Sting, and Seal, the sisters play their own instruments and write their own music, a fact that goes far with fans and critics alike. Not that success happened overnight. "We started picking up the guitar when we were eleven and thirteen," AJ explains. "That is when we got our Fender acoustics and we started playing on that. We started writing about six months later, after we had gotten in a good core of lessons."

Aly and AJ are definitely cute and stylish, with their golden coifs and casually hip fashion sense. But it's their God-given musical genius that sets them apart from other would-be pop sensations of the day. Their talents were on full display that Easter Sunday on the White House lawn. With their usual energy and flair, the sisters hit every high note of the national anthem, much to the delight of the crowd on hand.

Let's face it, though: You've got to have more than looks and talent to make it to the White House. Britney Spears and Lindsay Lohan can carry a tune, too, but you don't see them hanging out in the Oval Office much. This is where Aly and AJ really stand out from their pop peers in the music industry.

More than pretty faces singing catchy jingles, the Michalka sisters are genuine role models. You won't find them at the center of tabloid magazine scandals (unlike *some* teen icons we know). For Aly and AJ, music is not about fame, fortune, and nonstop partying. It's about self-expression, a way to spread the positive message that they carry in their hearts. "Our music I feel is a way of expressing ourselves through song and through our lyrics," Aly reflects. "AJ and I don't keep a diary or a journal, but our music is like an open diary to our fans. It is definitely very personal, and it has messages in there that we feel strongly about as well as topics we know people our age are going through and will be going through."

In "Rush," a track from their hit debut album *Into the Rush*, Aly and AJ encourage listeners to "Be every color that you are." During an interview with *Blender* magazine, Aly explained how the notions of dignity and self-belief are behind every song on the album. "It's just positive, uplifting messages," she said. AJ echoes this idea, urging fans to go after their dreams, even when the odds seem insurmountable. "If there is something you want to do in your life and you are really passionate about it, you should go for it 100 percent."

Is it any wonder that the White House invited Aly and AJ to perform at the Easter Egg Roll? After all, George Bush has always been a big fan of family values. The platform helped get him elected president not once, but twice.

As Aly and AJ wrapped up the singing of the national anthem, you can almost picture President Bush smiling and humming along. Of course, he's a pretty busy guy, so by the time the song was over, he'd already been ushered back inside. But that wasn't going to stop the Michalkas from getting their moment with the president. Not that they were pushy or anything. They were just, well, a little confused. "We kind of didn't really listen to direction, by accident," Aly told *Good Morning America*. Instead of exiting the stage, "we went back inside where [President Bush] was meeting," she continued.

Unannounced guests at the White House are usually enough to send in an army of Secret Service agents. But something about Aly and AJ seemed to assure everyone that the commander in chief wasn't in harm's way. In fact, President Bush greeted the gals like old friends! "He was so nice and gave us a huge hug after our performance," AJ recalls. "It was so cool. This was a huge moment in our lives that we will never forget. We cried after we performed."

Most performers can only dream about making it to the White House. Yet there was Aly, only seventeen years old at that time, and AJ, who had celebrated her fifteenth birthday just six days earlier, getting bear hugs from the president. Obviously, the Michalka sisters are not your average pop stars. "That's the first time it really hit us," AJ admits.

Since that April afternoon in 2006, Aly and AJ have only gotten bigger and better. They now have tons of acting credits to go along with their many musical accomplishments. And they're just getting started! More albums and acting gigs are already in the works, plus there's talk of everything from Aly & AJ clothing lines to video games. "I can see them in five years selling out arenas," says Bob Cavallo, chairman of Hollywood Records and the man who would give the sisters their first major record deal.

Aly and AJ are definitely destined for greatness. But to truly understand where they're headed, it's important to appreciate where they came from. *Amped Up* is their story, from their early years in Seattle up to and beyond that day at the White House when the president of the United States dropped everything to show that he, too, was ready to give it up for Aly and AJ.

CHAPTER TWO:
Twins, Two Years Apart

If you have a sister or a brother, you know that siblings can be both a blessing and a curse. Sure, it's great to have an ally in the house, especially when the 'rents start acting all unreasonable. But there are definitely moments when the thought of being an only child sounds pretty great (like when they "borrow" your favorite shirt!).

Mark and Carrie Michalka probably weren't too concerned with the concept of sibling rivalry when they decided to start a family back in the late eighties. Like most young couples, they were just trying to make ends meet. Mark earned an honest living from his small commercial contracting company, while Carrie added to the family income by working as a singer in several local bands.

Between the two paychecks, the Michalkas had socked away enough money to start a nice household in Torrance,

California. This bustling city is located in the southwestern, or "South Bay," region of Los Angeles County. Torrance is not exactly small-town America (in fact it's the 34th largest city in the enormous state of California), but it's definitely a desirable place to live. In fact, the town's high school served as the facade in two hit television shows, *Beverly Hills, 90210* and *Buffy the Vampire Slayer*, as well as one major movie, *She's All That*.

All in all, the Michalkas must have been super-excited when they got the news in the summer of 1988 that a baby was on the way. As the couple spent the next nine months preparing for their new life, they probably thought a lot about what their firstborn would be like. Carrie once worked as a cheerleader for the Los Angeles Raiders, so she could be forgiven for thinking her child might have some serious charisma. Mark, meanwhile, putting in long hours on construction sites, probably envisioned a son or daughter with lots of discipline and a solid work ethic. As fate would have it, they'd both get their wish!

Alyson Renae was born on March 25, 1989. So began a very joyous time in the Michalka household. Not only was Alyson healthy, she was beautiful, too, with big, blue-green eyes and golden tresses. She also had a bubbly personality. In fact, she was so friendly that before long she was going by the nickname Aly, which is a lot more fitting than the more formal-sounding Alyson.

Aly's early years were about as happy as could be. The house was filled with lots of music, and there were many trips to the Pacific Ocean, especially since Redondo Beach, Hermosa Beach, and Manhattan Beach were all just a short drive away. Still, as much as Carrie and Mark doted on Aly, it was clear that their toddler had lots more energy to give. What she really needed was a steady playmate.

As luck would have it, just two years after Carrie and Mark learned that they were expecting for the first time, they got news that a second child was on the way. Once again, they spent the fall and winter months getting ready for a newborn.

The big day came on April 10, 1991, when Carrie gave birth to the Michalka's second daughter, whom they christened Amanda Joy. It must have felt like déjà vu. Just like her sister, Amanda had beautiful, catlike eyes, blond hair, and the same sparkling personality. As with Aly, the latest addition to the family needed a more playful nickname. Before long, she would be known only as AJ, short for Amanda Joy.

From the very beginning, Aly and AJ were practically inseparable, so much so that it was often hard to tell who was who. In fact, the two sisters started to think of themselves as "the first set of twins to be born two years apart." Though the Michalka girls must have had plenty of other friends in the neighborhood, they really only needed each other. "My best friend? It's Aly," AJ told *Newsday*. "Yes, we are always together," AJ confirmed.

The fact that they share the same star sign, Aries, may have something to do with Aly and AJ's bond. If you're into reading horoscopes, you know that people born under the Aries sign have extremely exciting, infectious personalities. They're always at the front of the pack, whether in the classroom or during team sports.

With two Aries under one roof, there was never a dull moment in the Michalka household. The sisters entertained themselves with a lot of the usual activities. "Aly and I played with dolls every day," AJ recalls fondly. Even then, each of the sisters had her designated role in the partnership—often with pretty comical results. "Aly was the one that dressed them up and got them all ready," AJ continues. "She did their hair and wardrobe and I would be the one who set up the game. I would put the house together and would say, 'Who are you going to play? Are you going to play the mom?' Because I have such a low voice, I would usually play the dad. I would be, like, 'Aly I don't want to play the guy.' She was, like, 'You have to.' I was, like, 'Okay, fine.' Aly had a really high voice, so she would play the daughter. It was hilarious!"

Despite all the fun Aly and AJ had playing with dolls, it wasn't long before they discovered a love for putting on live performances. "AJ and I have just always loved performing and just being in front of an audience and stuff, but it really started at a very young age," Aly told the *Toronto Sun*.

The girls developed an early knack for self-promotion. "Another cool memory is us making homemade tickets at home and putting on concerts for neighbors," Aly says. AJ agrees. "That was so much fun. Aly would cut them out and I would put things on them. We would invite neighbors and friends. We would be, like, 'Hey guys, want to see us perform?' We had a dance routine. It was so funny!"

The sisters definitely took advantage of every opportunity

to put on a show, even at church. "For me, the thing that stands out the most is a duet that Aly and I did at church," AJ admits. "That was really cool because that was the first time we started performing together. We were in matching dresses and we were really little. To look back on it is really sweet because that is where Aly and AJ originate."

While Carrie and Mark couldn't have been surprised by their daughters' theatricality, they knew enough not to push the girls too hard. "It wasn't forced at all," Carrie told the *Tulsa World*, when asked how Aly and AJ became interested in entertainment. "I wanted them to learn an instrument, and they just chose the piano. They have been playing it since the time Aly was around six. And they have been performing so much over the years, it just came naturally to them."

The fact that Carrie used to be in a rock band herself must have made her proud of her daughters' burgeoning talents. Plus there were the years she spent in front of the camera every Sunday cheering on the Los Angeles Raiders. Not everyone considers cheerleading a legitimate form of entertainment, but it's actually a lot harder than it looks!

Aly and AJ definitely inherited their mom's talent.

As they got older, it became clear that they inherited their dad's discipline and dedication, too, especially when it came to making music. "AJ and I have been singing earlier than acting," Aly told ChristianityToday.com. "Ever since I can remember we were putting on music shows when the relatives would come over to the house, and practicing songs our mom would sing at church. AJ and I wanted to be like her when we were younger, so it really came from that. It's amazing when that transforms into something and you think, 'Wow, oh my gosh, God had that all planned!'"

The Michalkas are a devout, churchgoing family, but even with God on their side, Aly and AJ still had to convince their parents to let them go after their dream. "They were a little hesitant in the sense that our parents didn't really want us to be in the [entertainment] business," AJ says. "That was what they were weird about, in a good way. They really wanted us to live normal lives, which is great." Still, Aly's and AJ's passion proved pretty hard to ignore. "They knew Aly and I had so much passion and drive for it that they were, like, 'We can't stop this. This is literally a machine that our kids are driving and we can't stop that.' They recognized that, which I feel a lot of parents might not. So I give them credit for that for recognizing what we wanted to do in our lives and they just let us go for it."

Once the Michalka sisters got the green light from mom and dad, there was no stopping them. Aly officially started her acting career in elementary school, when she appeared in church productions of the musicals *Jailhouse Rock* and A *Time to Remember*. She was also proving to be a pretty talented artist. In fourth grade, she entered and won a contest run by Hallmark, the greeting card company. Her hand-drawn picture of angles in heaven was actually in the Christmas card lineup that year!

By this time, the Michalka family had relocated from Torrance to Woodinville, a suburb of Seattle, Washington. Unlike sunny Southern California, Seattle is known for its rainy weather. But Aly's and AJ's spirits weren't dampened by the move. In fact, they only seemed to blossom more! "Seattle was beautiful," AJ recalls. "It was really great to grow up in a place like Woodinville. We made a lot of great friends there and it was a really great family life. There is something about Woodinville that brings families really close. It was a really good place to grow up. The house that we lived in when we lived there was beautiful. We had this huge playhouse. The backyard was way big. Aly and I would play games out there. We had a big tree that we would put stuffed animals in."

Seattle was good for their careers, too. AJ was clearly following in her sister's footsteps, even appearing in some of the same musicals, including *Jailhouse Rock*. By the time she turned nine, AJ had also kicked off her career as a model, appearing in ads for companies like Disney, Mattel, Playmates Toys, Zutopia, and American Girl. That last gig was probably her favorite. "I was Kirsten, an American Girl doll," she says. "That was so cool because I was a huge fan of the dolls. To be in one in the print ads was huge." But really, AJ could have been modeling for a car commercial and she would have enjoyed it. "I love being in the hair and makeup chair. That is one of my favorite parts. Aly is a little fidgety in the hair chair, but I love it. I like makeup probably better than hair, but it is fun for me. I like seeing what each artist does. For them, that's their work." As if all that wasn't enough, she landed her first national television commercial on her very first audition!

Even as Aly and AJ continued to get acting and modeling gigs, their love of music kept growing. Fortunately, the family had moved to a music lover's paradise. Seattle rocks as hard as any city in America, rivaling places such as Austin, Nashville, and New York. When Aly and AJ arrived in the nineties, the city by the sea was home to the grunge music scene, thanks to the legendary Kurt Cobain and his rock band Nirvana, as well as groups like Pearl Jam and Soundgarden.

Aly and AJ definitely like to rock, so they probably listened to grunge. But Seattle had plenty of other musical influences for them to draw upon. Ann and Nancy Wilson from the eighties rock band Heart are from a suburb of the city called Bellevue. Aly and AJ were really into Heart's edgy, guitar-heavy sound, and the fact that a pair of sisters led the band appealed to them as well. Of course, they listened to bands from outside the Seattle area. "We listen to all sorts of music," AJ says. "We are very open to what we listen to. We are into a lot of different styles. We listen to Bob Marley all the time. We love Bob Marley. His records are really cool summer records. We have grown up on the Beach Boys."

Anyone growing up in and around Seattle in the nineties couldn't help but be into music. If you tuned in to the 2007 season of *American Idol* (and who didn't!), you know that runner-up Blake Lewis was raised just outside of the city. Blake is a little bit older than Aly and AJ, but he definitely has the same star power. Unfortunately, there was no such thing as *American Idol* when the Michalka girls decided to seriously pursue stardom. Instead, they would have to go about things the old-fashioned way, through hard work, determination, and just a little bit of luck. Fortunately, their amazing acting talents were already starting to open a lot of doors. But you might be surprised to learn that it was younger sister AJ who would be the first to go storming through them.

CHAPTER THREE

Little Sister Leads the Way

Everyone in AJ's family, as well as the church they attended each Sunday, knew she had talent. They had seen her belt out tunes fearlessly as the lead in musicals and other performances. But it was far from certain that she would take her abilities much farther than the walls of her parish. It wasn't a matter of her being shy or uncomfortable in the very adult world of show business. AJ had proved she was a total pro with her modeling gigs for magazine covers and all sorts of advertising campaigns. It might seem glamorous posing for a photographer and having your picture plastered all over stores, but the work behind the image can be quite uncomfortable. After hair and makeup, sitting under hot lights for hours, and photographers barking demands, even a model kid could really lose it. AJ always kept her cool, which showed she had the right temperament for basking in the limelight.

Still, there are loads of beautiful girls with talent and the desire to work really, really hard who never make it as actresses. There has to be the exact-right mix of luck, perseverance, sparkle, and magic to make everything click. It also doesn't hurt if you have a perky personality and infectious smile, just like AJ does. Casting directors recognized a star right away when they saw her. That's how AJ nailed her very first audition for a national commercial.

After winning her first part on the commercial, AJ was never without acting offers again. She landed her first role on a TV show, *Passions*, in 2002, when she was only eleven years old. On the whole, soap operas are a great training ground for actresses just starting out. First off, they are on five days a week, so that means a lot of acting! The people starring in these daytime dramas need to learn new scripts almost every day and large sections of dialogue on the fly since writers can be rewriting passages up until the last moment. They also have to be comfortable portraying a wide range of emotions since there's no lack of tragedy, passion, and betrayal on these shows. An actress can be in a coma in one episode and cheating her twin sister out of a massive fortune in the next. There's no predictability and absolutely no room for prima donnas on a soap set. There's just too much work to be done.

AJ only appeared on *Passions* for one episode, which first aired on May 7, 2002, so she didn't have much of an opportunity to prove herself. But it was a start. "It is so interesting being on a soap opera because it is so different. That was pretty cool," she says. Certainly if she had been frightened by all the cameras, lights, props, and actors moving around, her mom would have never let her continue acting. Of course that didn't happen; AJ was a real pro.

AJ's next role proved to be an important milestone in her career. She finally landed a coveted spot on prime-time television. Obviously it's fantastic to appear anywhere on the small screen if you are an actress, but prime time is the most competitive part of network TV because that's when most people tune in. The process just for a show to make it into one of those coveted time slots is long and grueling. Says AJ: "Life on a TV [show's] set is definitely hard work because you are up really really early for an early call time and then you go pretty much straight to hair and makeup, then wardrobe, then you rehearse and then you film. It is definitely a pretty crazy process. You can shoot for a long time."

That's assuming the show is even picked up by a network. First, producers need to pitch the idea to a board full of executives from one of the five major networks. If they pass that hurdle, they then get the go-ahead to make a pilot, which is the first episode of the show. The pilot also needs to give a general feel of where the series will go and what viewers can expect when they tune in. After they cast the pilot and shoot it, the show has to be presented to the executives again. There are many more pilots produced every year than shows on television. If the network likes what they see, then they order episodes of the series and put it on the air.

The same year she appeared on *Passions*, AJ found herself on the prime-time lineup for the WB, a network that no longer exists. She was psyched to be on *Birds of Prey*, a sci-fi adventure series that took up where Batman and Catwoman left off. In this series, the daughter of the two superheroes, whose name is Huntress, follows in her parents' footsteps. She disguises herself and spends her nights maintaining peace and order. She has two gal pals in her heroic hobby: Oracle, who once went by the name Batgirl, and Dinah, a runaway whose special ability allows her to explore people's minds. "That was a really cool show to be on because it was such an original story line and everyone was really cool," AJ says.

Unfortunately, the show didn't last very long. *Birds of Prey*, like so many prime-time shows, was quickly given the axe. It aired its last episode on February 19, 2003, only four months and thirteen episodes after it began. Still, with her first prime-time show under her belt, AJ had progressed from her one-shot stint on *Passions*.

AJ continued to move quickly. With her next gig, she took yet another major career leap. CBS offered her a reoccurring role as the character Shannon Gressler on its prime-time drama *The Guardian*. This was a lot of responsibility for young AJ. Premiering September 25, 2001, *The Guardian* tells the story of Nick Fallin, a corporate attorney in Pittsburgh, Pennsylvania, who finds himself on the wrong side of the law after a drug conviction. As part of his punishment, Nick (who is played by the dashing actor Simon Baker) is sentenced to 1,500 hours of community service with Legal Services of Pittsburgh, where he represents children in the welfare system. That's a far cry from the powerful, rich clients he tends to at the corporate law firm where his father (played by Dabney Coleman) is president. But it's all part of Nick's journey as he gets off drugs and learns to truly care about those in need. Just the kind of message AJ could really get behind!

AJ appeared on fifteen episodes of *The Guardian* before it ended on May 4, 2004. During that time, a major TV legend showed up on the set to guest-star in several episodes. The star was none other than Farrah Fawcett. If you don't know who she is, dust off your television encyclopedia because she was one of the hottest stars on the small screen during the 1970s. That's when she appeared on the original *Charlie's Angels* series as one of the crime-fighting angels. As the blonde one of the three ladies, Farrah stood out. And practically every girl growing up at that time wanted her thick, feathered, seriously dirty blonde locks. With her short-shorts, knee-high socks, groovy T-shirt, and skateboard, Farrah became a style icon of her day. Boys drooled over a famous poster of her, which sold over seven million copies, and girls were forever trying to copy that famous hairstyle. On *The Guardian*, Farrah played AJ's grandmother in several episodes. She was also the love interest for Nick's dad, Burton Fallin, played by Dabney Coleman. Farrah still gets the guy!

It was definitely a great experience working with such a legendary actress. "Farrah was so sweet to me," AJ says. "She gave me one of her first pieces of work for her art, a beautiful bracelet with faces on it. She sent me a huge letter when we first started working together. She would leave really supportive messages on my phone. She was really cool. She encouraged me to keep going and supported me in my craft. It was neat to have that support off the get-go. She was serious about her work, which taught me a lot."

Farrah Fawcett wasn't the only brush AJ would have with television history. Right after *The Guardian* ended, she had a chance to act on what critics have called "the greatest soap opera of all time." If you have a parent or older sibling who is addicted to soaps, you know right away that the critics are talking about *General Hospital*. AJ appeared as a girl named Ashley on three episodes of the soap, which has been on the air since April 1, 1963. That's over forty years! *GH*, as it is known for short, is ABC's longest-running dramatic serial. It's won tons of awards—including a record-breaking seven Daytime Emmy Awards for Outstanding Drama Series—and was called by *TV Guide*, in its 40th Anniversary Special Edition, the "All-Time Best Daytime Soap." That's pretty lofty praise. But perhaps the best sign of its success is the constant stream of stars it has had wander through the fictional upstate New York town of Port Charles, where the show is set. Over the years, such bold-faced names as Demi Moore, Elizabeth Taylor, Ricky Martin, and John Stamos have entered into the passion, lies, and adventure of *GH*'s intricate story lines. So AJ was in good company when she signed on to be part of the celebrity tradition!

In 2004, AJ was superbusy. She played Shannon on *The Guardian* and appeared on *General Hospital*. That was just the start. AJ also acted on a Fox comedy, *Oliver Beene*, about the life of eleven-year-old Oliver, played by Grant Rosenmeyer. Grant is a talented young actor who made his film debut in the critically acclaimed feature film *The Royal Tenenbaums*, about a super-quirky family. His crazy curls stand out for anyone who saw the film, and his role earned him a Young Artist Award for Best Performance in a Feature Film—Young Actor Age Ten or Under.

The comedy takes place during 1962, and poor Oliver's world is a mess. If this is any indication of how dire things are for the kid, his dad, Jerry, played by Grant Shaud, is a dentist who enjoys passing Sunday afternoons by drilling his own kids' teeth. Yikes! The half-hour program, in which AJ played a character named Bonnie for eight episodes, depicts what it was like growing up in the 1960s. Some things, such as the president and fashions, were totally different. But some things never change: Oliver has a teacher who hates his guts, a girl who has a massive crush on him, and another girl he wished did.

AJ really took to her cast mates during the taping of the show. "I became friends with everyone on *Oliver Beene* because we were all the same age. We would hang out all the time. We would all eat in our trailers together. We would have lunch every day together. We would leave the set at the same time. We had recess on set during lunch break. The soundstages had bikes and stuff. It takes place in the sixties. We would have a bunch of props from set and we would ride our bikes around the Fox lot."

Unfortunately, Fox pulled the sitcom off the air after a little more than six months. Oh well for Oliver. *Oliver Beene*'s demise didn't slow down AJ. In the same year, AJ struck out on a much darker note when she accepted the role of another Ashley, this time on the HBO drama *Six Feet Under*. This was a real departure for the young actress, who had mainly stuck to soap operas, sitcoms, and good-natured network dramas. HBO is known as one of the edgiest channels on cable and is responsible for some of the darkest, most violent, and most startling shows around. "[The experience] was really, really cool," AJ says. "It was amazing being part of such a great show with such an amazing story line and cast. That show is so clever and interesting. I was actually on one of the last seasons. It was cool to come on then. Everybody was super nice, especially for having such a successful show on the air, everyone was super cool."

HBO has a reputation for award-winning programming— adored by both critics and fans—such as *The Sopranos*, *Sex and the City*, and *The Wire*. *Six Feet Under*, created by Oscar-winning screenwriter Alan Ball, was no exception. It revolves around the Fishers, a family who runs a very unusual family business, a funeral parlor. But the dead are the least of the Fisher family's problems. This is one seriously dysfunctional clan. That's what makes for interesting TV, right? *Six Feet Under* had a devoted viewership throughout its entire run, from the premiere on June 3, 2001, until its final episode on August 21, 2005.

AJ appeared in one episode, "Falling into Place," which first aired June 13, 2004. Needless to say, the episode dealt with a lot of dark subjects and, of course, a lot of death. *Six Feet Under* might not have been a perfect fit for AJ's bubbly and fun personality, but the guest role meant a lot of exposure. Not that she really needed it. Within two short years, AJ had become a real rarity in Hollywood: an actress with steady work.

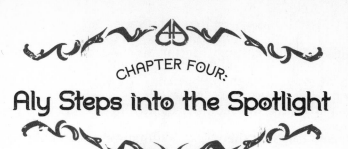

CHAPTER FOUR

Aly Steps into the Spotlight

AJ's career had taken off, but what about Aly? These two sisters and best friends do practically everything together. Was AJ going to become a star and just leave her big sister in the dust? Fat chance. Aly is way too talented to leave all the acting to her little sis.

Sure enough, it didn't take much for Aly to follow in her little sister's footsteps. Talk about a role reversal! She broke out onto the acting scene with a bang. Aly landed a lead role on the Disney TV series *Phil of the Future*. "*Phil of the Future* was how I got known," she explains. "What a way to start out your career, being part of such a great big company that is so successful and is really able to launch you. The fan base that I got from that is something that has carried over into my music career."

Still, it's lucky that Aly even got the part at all. As she

explains, "I was going to a workshop and after going for a little bit, the casting director for the series was actually coaching the workshop. She said, 'Aly you should go in for this part Keely.'" At first, Aly balked. "They had seen over a thousand girls for this role." But finally she relented. "I went in a couple days after the work shop . . . We did a bunch of fun exercises, really weird stuff . . . I was literally in there for three hours, throwing around paper and mugging for the camera, talking, it was really fun. I didn't think I was really going to get it. It was between me and another girl, and I didn't have any credits. This was a series regular and why would they hire me for such a big role?" The casting agents obviously didn't share Aly's reservations. "I was with my dad at work," she recalls. "I was just running errands with him and my dad got the phone call. He said my manager wanted to talk to me. I found out right there and then, in a bank, and I was freaked out. I practically dropped my lollipop. I had to get into wardrobe the next day, and the day after that we got right on set and it was showtime, so it was wild. Everyone was, like, 'Yay, we found our Keely!'"

Phil of the Future wasn't just any old TV Show. The sci-fi series was created by Douglas Tuber, the same man behind the hit TV show *Lizzie McGuire*, which catapulted its leading actress Hilary Duff into megastardom. Douglas didn't create *Lizzy McGuire*, which began in 2001 on the Disney Channel. But he helped turn the series into a runaway hit. On the show, Hilary played an ordinary seventh-grader dealing with ordinary issues, such as what to wear to school or how to put her archrivals in place. Of course Hilary is anything but ordinary and she can credit the show with her extraordinary status. During its four-year run, it became the Disney Channel's flagship show and really set the tone for all the programs that came after it. A movie based on the TV show, *The Lizzie McGuire Movie*, hit theaters on May 2, 2003. So many *Lizzie* fans turned out to see the good-natured girl on the big screen that the film was second in the box office its opening week, right behind the gigantic blockbuster *X2: X-Men United*. The movie was only the start of the spin-offs. There were Lizzie McGuire books, a Lizzie McGuire doll, Lizzie McGuire video games, Lizzie McGuire bedroom sets, board games, and the list goes on and on. *Fortune* magazine estimated that in 2003, all this *Lizzie McGuire* merchandise earned the Walt Disney Company a whopping $100 million! The show's influence spread far and wide. In an episode of *The Simpsons,* even Marge and Homer went to see *The Lizzie McGuire Movie.*

With Douglas at the helm of *Phil of the Future*, the Disney Channel was hoping for another hit, Lizzie McGuire-style. The show's plot revolves around the Diffys, a family who is from the year 2121. (The production company that made the kids' show is aptly named 2121 Productions.) When Dad rents a time machine for the family vacation, everyone is psyched. But during the little jaunt, the machine malfunctions and they land in the year 2004. The vehicle breaks, and they get stuck in the twenty-first century. What a drag! The Diffys are undaunted and spend the series trying to repair their time machine to return home and to the year 2121.

The main character, Phil Diffy, played by supercute Ricky Ullman, spends a lot of his time trying to hide the fact that he's from the future while his silly dad, Lloyd, played by Craig Anton, tries to get that darned time machine up and running. Although Lloyd's an engineer in his future real life, he works at the Mantis hardware store while they remain stuck. Life in their average suburban town, Pickford, is anything but normal. The present is especially hard on

Phil's mom, Barbara, played by Lise Simms. Part robot, Barbara can never cook a proper meal because she's used to spraying food from a can. Little sister Pim, played by Amy Bruckner, makes her stay in the twenty-first century quite interesting with loads of practical jokes on her older bro and the vice principal of her school! There aren't many kids who could get away with that.

Aly played Keely Teslow, Phil's best friend who eventually becomes his girlfriend. The costume and hair and makeup departments had a field day with adorable Aly. They gave her many different and wild hairstyles as well as bold wardrobe choices, which became a notable part of the show. It's only natural that they would want to play to Aly's strengths, and her pretty face is certainly one of them. Keely steals Phil's heart, but she's also the only person who's in on the Diffy family secret that they are from the future. While it's hard to keep that to herself, there are also benefits to knowing the secret. Sometimes she takes advantage of Phil's futuristic gadgets to help with her homework. In one episode, Keely gets to glimpse into the future and learns her dream of becoming a news reporter will indeed happen. That's pretty cool. Despite Phil's unusual background, he and Keely face all the things normal teenagers face: They have to do homework, put up with bullies, get crushes, and deal with parents. That stuff never changes no matter what year you are in.

Taping *Phil of the Future* was a blast for Aly. She was constantly hanging out in her cast mates' rooms, playing pranks, and getting piggyback rides around the set, though getting into costume was maybe the most fun of all. "I was really close with hair, makeup, and my wardrobe stylist," she says. "I was really close with my makeup artist. We always had our inside jokes. She gave me face massages in the morning. I always had my plate of bacon in the morning, and my juice that was a mixture of five different juices. We all had our own little things that made us our own unique selves on set."

The show premiered on June 18, 2004, and by October of 2004, it was the number one show with kids, in its time slot. *Phil of the Future* had about four million viewers tuning in for each episode! That's a lot of people watching. In its second season, the sci-fi series began to garner critical acclaim and industry recognition. The Writers Guild of America nominated the episode "Broadcast Blues," which was written by David Steven Cohen, for an award in the Children's Episode and Specials category. The Directors Guild of America also nominated *Phil of the Future* for the episode entitled "Not So Great Great Great Grandpa." It happened to be directed by Fred Savage, who was not only a coproducer on *Phil of the Future,* but also a child star, just like AJ and Aly.

Fred had been a household name back in the late eighties and early nineties when he starred on the megahit show *The Wonder Years,* about what else: a normal kid growing up with normal problems. After the show ended in 1993, Fred found another passion: directing. He began this new career by directing episodes of over a dozen series for young people, including *That's So Raven* and *Hannah Montana* for the Disney Channel. Obviously, Fred was able to put his success as an actor to good use by translating his experience on set into a new role as director. He could also understand what the young actors were going through because he had gone through it himself. The more sensitivity a director has, the better the show or film.

Besides a great cast, talented writers, and a wonderful director, *Phil of the Future* was a hit because of the zany gadgets peppered throughout the show. There were the gizmos good for fashion, such as the Dress-Me Hoop that automatically dresses anyone who walks through the hoop. Who wouldn't kill for that tool on school-week mornings? There was also a gadget that turned completely messed-up hair neat and straight in an instant. Good-bye, hair dryers and brushes! But those things hardly compare to the Skyak, a Jet Ski that flies in the air, or the Replicator, which can clone a person. If you had one of those, you could go to class and go shopping or play sports—at the same time! As for Aly, if she could have one gadget from the show, she says, "I would use the Wizard the most because the Wizard does just about anything. It can make you food right then and there. It can help with your homework. It can change your clothes."

Unfortunately, there was no gadget that could keep *Phil of the Future* on TV forever. The series aired its last episode on August 19, 2006. In that farewell broadcast, Phil and Keely are voted "cutest couple" by all their classmates, and the friends finally decide to start dating. It seems like a happy ending, but not for long. The time machine has been fixed, and Phil's dad, Lloyd, realizes that if they return home, the Diffy family can never return to the twenty-first century. Phil and Keely's love is doomed! Although those who care about the couple try to destroy the machine so he can remain with his sweetie, Phil puts a stop to it. He can't ask his family to stay forever in a place where they don't belong. The only consolation Phil and Keely get is one good-bye kiss before he hops on the time machine to zoom back to the future with his family.

The ending of the series was a bittersweet moment in Aly's career, especially given how suddenly it all happened. "It was weird because we didn't get to say good-bye to anyone properly because we thought we were going to come back," she says. "It was the second season, and I was, like, 'I'll see you guys again soon and it's all good,' and we never came back. We didn't get to have a final hurrah. I am glad it worked out the way it did, because AJ and I would not have been able to go on tour like we did. It would have affected our music. It worked out for the good of everybody."

A lot of fans were sad to see *Phil of the Future* end after forty-three episodes. People even petitioned to bring the show back through the website www.savepotf.org, which was led by the same group that got the cartoon *Kim Possible* back on the air after the Disney Channel canceled it in 2005. Fans were crazy for *Kim Possible*, an animated series about a teenage crime fighter who travels the globe to battle villains and rescue victims but is always back home in time to complete her homework and fulfill her duties as captain of the cheerleading squad. They lobbied so hard that Disney reversed its own policy to cancel any show, no matter how popular, after sixty-five episodes and wound up ordering a fourth season of *Kim Possible*.

The warriors didn't have the same success with *Phil of the Future* and it stayed off the air permanently. But two years is an amazing run for a series in the fickle and quick-lived world of television. Plus, the Disney Channel doesn't scrimp on the reruns, so *Phil* lovers can often catch a glimpse of their favorite characters.

Aly certainly didn't shed any tears. This is a girl who can roll with the punches, so she quickly set her sights on other exciting projects. Aly was so talented, pretty, and full of energy that it wasn't long before she was scooped up by another director.

Her next acting gig was *Now You See It*, an original made-for-TV movie for the Disney Channel. Aly left behind the sci-fi gadgets of *Phil of the Future*, but she didn't roam far. *Now You See It* had its fair share of fantastic features. In it, Aly plays a girl named Allyson Miller (responding to that name didn't take much acting!), a teen producer who sets out to run a reality show starring a top-notch kid magician. In her search for such a star, she comes across Danny Sinclair, played by Johnny Pacar. He's amazing with tricks—almost *too* amazing. But Danny must compete against two other young magicians, Brandon (Gabriel Sunday) and Zoey (Amanda Shaw). The show host and master magician Max knows there is something different and unique about Danny. Soon, Allyson knows it, too. Danny's not any ordinary performer—he's got real magical powers.

Landing a part on a Disney movie is a thrill in itself, but with this project Aly got the chance to work with one of the top actors of stage and screen living today. The part of Max was played by Frank Langella, who has won two Tony Awards and was nominated for many more. He made a name for himself in the title role of Dracula on Broadway, where he wowed audiences with his creepy but dynamic presence. His talent hasn't been confined to Broadway. Although he largely stayed away from film and TV in order to pursue theater, Frank has been in *Law & Order: Special Victims Unit*, *Star Trek*, *Superman Returns*, and many other popular TV shows. His unique ability to play both villains and comic characters ensured that a wide variety of roles continuously came his way.

Most actors would have killed someone for a chance to work with Langella. Meanwhile, Aly had the opportunity to act alongside this world-class performer and it was only her second time at bat. She definitely took a lot of notes. "He was eccentric and offbeat," she recalls. "Just the way he talked and his hand movements. He always had lunch in his trailer by himself—those kinds of things. He is an actor who has been working for years and he has his thing down."

Filming *Now You See It* was an all-around magical experience for Aly. "We filmed in New Orleans and had such a good time. We had a great cast. Part of that cast were actual magicians, so they would do magic tricks in their rooms for us. We would go down to the French Quarter and go shopping, and we would watch scary movies late at night and freak each other out. That was one of the best movie experiences that I had. I grew to love New Orleans and just the whole vibe, the music and the history." Little did she know that her newly beloved city would soon be ravaged by one of the worst natural disasters in American history. "It was sad because when we came back out on tour later on after Katrina," she explains, "it was so different than when I was there and everybody was so happy out and about and it was kind of empty and torn down. It made me sad. That is why AJ and I wanted to write a song inspired by Katrina and how it made us feel, and that song is called "Tears." "Tears" is an exclusive track for Target on Aly and AJ's *Insomniatic* album.

The *Now You See It* movie premiered in the United States on January 14, 2005. The action-packed flick quickly went global, screening in Canada, Japan, the United Kingdom, Italy, and Latin America. Now it was official: Aly had become a bona fide international star.

CHAPTER FIVE

Walking on Sunshine

The Michalka sisters were both seeing so much success as actresses at a time when most kids are only concerned with school cliques and figuring out math homework. What more could they want? But acting wasn't the be-all, end-all for these talented siblings. Put it this way: They never forgot about their first love.

Once upon a time, the entertainment industry was divided into neat categories. You were either a musician or an actor. Sure, there were exceptions, among them Elvis Presley and Judy Garland, but for the most part, crossover acts weren't the norm.

That was then. These days, if you can't sing *and* act *and* dance, your chances of making it big are severely limited. Fortunately, Aly and AJ have it all going on. So even though they were finding success as models and actresses, they never forgot about the music. In fact, singing stayed atop their list of passions. "You know acting is great, because you get a chance to create a character," AJ told the *Tulsa World*. "But if I had to choose, my first love would be music."

Aly and AJ had plenty of role models to look to as they started on their creative musical journey. "We really grew up around gospel music and Sting, The Police . . . We love singer-songwriters," Aly told the *South Bend Tribune*. In a separate interview with the *Home News Tribune,* she was even more emphatic about her and AJ's musical roots. "That's where it all started for us," she said. "Music is something we shared since we were kids in our bedroom. Music is what we love the most. We're not making music to advance our acting careers. Acting is great. You're playing somebody else. With music, it comes from your heart and soul. It's all you."

For the most part, musicians—like entertainers of old—fall into one of two categories: They're either performers or they're artists. The industry is teeming with performers, some of whom are truly gifted, oozing charisma all over the stage, but to be considered an artist, you need more than an awesome voice or acrobatic dance moves. In a word, you've got to have soul.

As you'll see, Aly and AJ were raised in an extremely spiritual environment. They attend church regularly, sure, but more than that, their parents brought them up to always know right from wrong. Carrie and Mark Michalka also taught their daughters to live by the golden rule: Do unto others as you would have done unto you. As a result, Aly and AJ are two of the most conscientious teenagers you'll ever meet.

When they finally decided to get serious about making music, these core values were the driving force behind their ambition. Aly was only thirteen at the time, and AJ just eleven, but they were wise beyond their years, and the lyrics they wrote proved it. "Aly and I are both listeners and we both like to reflect on what other people have to say," AJ admitted to *Newsday*. "We listen to what kids say, or teens and adults. We end up writing about that. We like to write about what has happened to us in our life."

From the very beginning, Aly and AJ definitely took songwriting very seriously. "The writing process is very random and spontaneous, extremely creative, and very passionate," explains Aly. "At times it can get really intense, and other times it can be very calming and liberating. We

Baby Amanda Joy
taking a nap.

ALy, age 2, Loved
to PLAy outside.

SisterLy Love.

AJ PLAying
DRess up.

AJ and ALY PLAYING with their DOLLS.

ALY was ready to swim!

AJ at a tap Dance Lesson.

Ahoy Matey—it's Pirate AJ and her dog Toby.

ALY and AJ making waves at the beach.

ALY PLaying in a piano recital when she was seven.

AJ Liked getting dirty when she played outside.

Both ALY and AJ
Love riding horses!

ALY and AJ go for
a ride on the beach.

AJ with Bandit and ALY with Saint in a Pet Store.

It's nap time for ALY, AJ, and their Dogs Saint, Bandit, Roadie, and Willow.

AJ and ALY on the red carpet with television host Larry King.

ALY and AJ in the studio in 2000.

ALY with her "Phil of the Future" co-star Ricky Ullman in NYC.

AJ on the set of "The Guardian."

AJ with Farrah Fawcett on the set of "The Guardian."

Aly working on a song.

ALY and AJ at the
White House to sing
the national anthem.

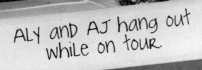

ALY and AJ hang out
while on tour.

Beautiful!

AJ and Aly at their
high school graduation.

ALY, Michael Trevino, AJ, and Chris Gallinger became friends while filming Cowbelles.

ALY and AJ pose in a vintage Mustang.

ALY experiences life on a farm with co-star Michael Trevino on the set of Cowbelles.

AJ with a calf on the set of the Disney Channel's made-for-TV movie, Cowbelles.

ALY AND AJ WEREN'T afraid to get DOWN AND DIRTY WHILE filming COWBELLES.

ALY and AJ at a
Live Performance.

The girls rockin'
out on stage.

ALY is amped up on tour.

ALY Jammin' on her guitar

AJ gives ALY a kiss at their joint 16th and 18th birthday party.

AJ getting into character on the set of Super Sweet Sixteen.

AJ hanging out with her co-stars on the set of *super sweet sixteen*.

ALY and co-star Regine Nehy get messy on the set of *super sweet sixteen*.

ALY as Taylor Tiara on the set of MTV's made-for-TV movie *super sweet sixteen*.

go through a bunch of different emotions while writing, and definitely have a lot of ups and downs."

Still, even though songwriting took the sisters into some dark territory, that's not to say they didn't have fun with the process. As a matter of fact, they often penned the lyrics in their pajamas! Plus, they were constantly drawing on others for inspiration, so music making was never a lonely experience. "We have written a song with our mom, and we have collaborated with other writers and producers," AJ explained to *Newsweek*. Having a mother who used to be a rocker herself (Carrie was in a Christian music band called The J.C. Band) really helped Aly and AJ focus on the music. "[Our mom] was a singer-songwriter," AJ said in the *Charlotte Observer*. "She's an amazing lyricist. We've been able to collaborate with her."

By 2003, after countless hours of hard work (with an acceptable amount of goofing off between songwriting sessions) Aly and AJ were finally finished with their first demo tape. The soulful sound that fans of Aly and AJ identify with so intensely was there from the beginning, starting with "Collapsed," which Aly referred to in the *Fort Lauderdale Sun-Sentinel* as "their first true song." It's all about the delicacy of relationships and that feeling of sadness we all feel when someone loved is lost forever. Here's a sample of the lyrics:

Why did I let you go
You're too good to be true
I messed it up and now I don't know what to do
We ran in circles and wasted time
From right to wrong
From right to wrong

The depth and soulfulness of "Collapsed" set the tone for the rest of the tracks on Aly and AJ's first album. "I really would say that the whole album is definitely a piece of our heart," Aly told the *Toronto Sun*. "It's definitely got some deep lyrics and some personal messages and meanings. AJ and I really like to it call it 'melodic rock.' It's really musically beautiful to listen to and the songs are really positive, too." By this time, the sisters had settled on a name for the album, one that captured its theme perfectly. As Aly explained, "I think *Into the Rush*, the name of the album, really kind of signifies what the album is about. We're in this rush together, AJ and I, and it's amazing."

The rush Aly describes can be felt up and down the album. Whether the tunes are fast and pop-like or slow and folksy, the lyrics almost always reflect life in a real and meaningful way. Relationships is one theme that Aly and AJ return to time and again; take the tune "Protecting Me," in which the sisters sing:

You listen to me when
I speak out loud and you
You know right when my heart's been bent
When my life's tumbling around
You take me off the ground
You tell me everything's OK

Whereas "Protecting Me" is very personal, other songs on *Into the Rush* are a comment on society at large. A lot of the times the lyrics are drawn from real-life experiences, which almost gives them the quality of a poem. "Every song is really special to me, just because they all have their own specific meaning," Aly told the *Toronto Sun*. Of course, some of the tunes cut closer to the bone than others. "One of the songs on the album is called "Sticks and Stones," and that's a song that I think a lot of kids and adults can relate to because it's about being bullied," she continued. "I think we all go through some kind of a phase where we are bullied and it's just a song I think can uplift you even when you're being bullied. It's an anthem for kids out there who are being made fun of or teased, which isn't cool. AJ and I have gone through it and it's terrible."

With "Sticks and Stones," Aly and AJ tackled one of the most serious issues facing teens today. Anyone who has ever been bullied will definitely relate to the track. But as serious as bullying is, it's nothing compared to the issue Aly and AJ tackled in their song "I Am One of Them," which confronts the terrifying issue of kidnapping, which was very prevalent in the news during the summer of 2002. Here's how the opening refrain goes:

I get in the car
Another tragic disaster
But I'm safe where I am
Yet another is captured
The traffic is stopped
The people just stare
Another alert does the kid have a prayer?
Life is not fair

"It is important to touch on those topics and even topics that might be something that isn't really talked about—a topic such as child kidnapping," says Aly, discussing the inspiration behind "I Am One of Them." "AJ and I wrote a song about it and we feel really strongly about keeping kids safe and being on the alert from predators. AJ and I wanted to write a song about how we felt about the situation and how we are one of them. We are one of those kids on the TV screen that are missing. We all could be up there."

One kidnapping is bad enough, but seeing the reports night after night on television that summer had a serious impact on Aly and AJ, especially when the horrific events were being caught on camera. "We really started to think it was becoming an epidemic, and then one day we heard a story of a girl who was kidnapped at a car wash—and they actually had footage from the security cameras of her being led off. It was absolutely mortifying seeing her."

Writing the music and lyrics for "I Am One of Them" was a therapeutic experience for Aly and AJ. It helped them come to terms with this very serious issue. But it also taught them the importance of rallying behind causes that you believe in. "AJ and I have always really felt strongly about missing children and that subject in general," Aly explained to ChristianityToday.com. "We want to bring awareness to children and parents and basically got so fed up one day that we had to do something. We're child safety advocates, we donate money to those causes and want people to know even the smallest amount of support can make a huge difference." They want kids to know how important it is to always tell your parents where you are going and to never take off with a stranger no matter what excuse he gives.

With *Into the Rush*, Aly and AJ were proving themselves to be serious artists. But they never took themselves so seriously that they forgot how to have fun. During breaks from their songwriting, they found plenty of time for all their favorite hobbies, whether dancing, cooking, riding horses and mountain bikes, reading books, or just hanging out with their dogs.

All in all, Aly and AJ were feeling pretty good about their first demo tape. But they still had to convince a music producer to get on board with it as well, which is a lot easier said than done. Fortunately, the success they'd been having in television promised to pave the way. Most important were the inroads they'd made with the Disney Company—in particular, Aly's success on the popular show *Phil of the Future*.

In the last decade or so, Disney has perfected the formula of using multiple platforms—television, movies, music, merchandising, video games, and more—to promote their performers. It's resulted in the creation of some of the biggest teen celebrities on the planet. But success is by no means guaranteed, so the Disney execs are extremely selective when choosing new talent to cultivate. "We still only sign artists we believe have a future, whether [with] Disney or not," Bob Cavallo, CEO of the Disney-owned Hollywood Records, told Billboard.com. "The first one was Hilary Duff, whose *Lizzie McGuire* became such a successful TV show and film that it became obvious the next step was to launch a Hilary Duff career. Let's face it, between her sound tracks and Hilary Duff records, she's sold over 13 million units."

As Cavallo and the rest of the Disney brass started searching for their next Hilary Duff, they had a lot of potential young stars to choose from. Names like Hayden Panettiere or Caleigh Peters must have popped up, but none of them had the multitalented appeal that's so essential to the Disney formula. Then, one day, Cavallo had the opportunity to meet face-to-face with Aly and AJ. With their gorgeous golden locks and cheery personalities, the sisters definitely had star potential. Plus, they had already proven their ability to shine in front of the camera. But could they sing?

In the fast-paced entertainment industry you don't get

a second chance to make a first impression. Fortunately, Aly and AJ had been preparing for this moment pretty much their entire lives—not that that made them any less anxious. "We were so nervous," AJ admits. "The crazy thing is that right before we played for them, Aly had the wrong string on one of her guitars. We slipped out and someone from Gerry's office ended up going out and getting a string before we got there. Aly and I were, like, 'We are freaking out!' Everyone was, like, 'Don't worry. It's okay.' Then we played."

Big-shot music industry executives like Bob Cavallo are pitched new acts every day, so it's pretty easy for them to tune out completely in those moments, thinking instead about when their next meeting is or what they're going to have for dinner that night. But as soon as Aly and AJ started strumming their guitars, Cavallo was rapt. He knew in an instant that he was looking at his next stars. "They were sitting on stools, playing five songs they wrote," Cavallo recalled in *Blender* magazine. "I signed them on the spot."

Cavallo loved the heart and soulfulness of Aly and AJ's music, but he knew that for their first album to be a success, it would have to include some lighter tracks. So he asked the sisters to cover a couple of classic, upbeat tunes. Aly and AJ quickly agreed. After all, they didn't want to depress their listeners with an album full of bullies and kidnappers. The first cover, called "Do You Believe in Magic," was originally released by the Lovin' Spoonful in 1965. It's definitely a happy track, though nothing compared to their second cover, the infectious, feel-good tune "Walking on Sunshine," made famous by Katrina and the Waves back in 1985.

The two cover tunes balanced out the heavier tracks on *Into the Rush*. And they gave Aly and AJ an opportunity to let their hair down and really have some fun. As Aly explained to ChristianityToday.com: "['Do You Believe in Magic'] was really neat for us and so much fun to sing! And 'Walking on Sunshine' is such a feel good summer song." In the *Home News Tribune*, Aly was even more enthusiastic about the cover tunes. "Both of those songs fit us so well," she said. "Both songs are classics. We relate to 'Walking on Sunshine.' We feel as teenagers that we're always walking on sunshine."

The album was complete! With the Disney machine behind them, Aly and AJ were one giant step closer toward becoming teen celebrity sensations. They put the finishing touches on *Into the Rush* and recorded the tracks in the studio. By 2005, the album was ready for release. Everyone involved had high hopes for its success. But the public can be pretty unpredictable, giving the cold shoulder to performers who are supposed to be sure things. So, on the eve of the release, Aly and AJ were understandably anxious. "We were so excited," says AJ. "I was, like, 'Oh my gosh our record just came out. Right when it turned midnight that day, I took my phone and recorded on my voice mail (I still have it). I was, like, 'Our record *Into the Rush* just dropped. I am so excited to see what happens.' That was it. I'll never forget that moment." As it turned out, AJ and Aly didn't need to be nervous. In a matter of months, the response to *Into the Rush* would have them walking on sunshine for real.

CHAPTER SIX

A Huge Rush in Sales

Into the Rush hit record stores on August 16, 2005. Aly was just sixteen at the time, while AJ was only fourteen. Even with the support of Disney, not to mention their own tremendous self-belief, the sisters were definitely sweating the release. "It was all new for us," Aly recalls. "We didn't know what to expect." Not only that, many a musical career is won (and lost) on the success of that first album.

But, as we all know now, they had nothing to worry about. From the very beginning, *Into the Rush* was a hit with both fans and critics. Music reviewers were quick to praise Aly and AJ's polished sound and mature songwriting, drawing comparisons to Stevie Nicks and Christine McVie from the hall of fame rock band Fleetwood Mac.

Within a few short months, *Into the Rush* had sold upward of 250,000 units, a figure that would climb to upward of one million in the first year. Aly and AJ knew they had talent, but nothing could have prepared them for this kind of reaction. "We were blown away," Aly admits. "The fans connected to us . . . We could definitely feel their energy and their passion. They definitely trusted in us, which was really neat. They connected with our honesty in our lyrics and in our emotional connection to the songs."

Before the Michalka sisters had time to soak in the excitement, though, Disney was already kicking its publicity machine into high gear. Encouraged by the early sales of the album, the company's first bold move was to pair Aly and AJ with another huge success, The Cheetah Girls.

Less than six months after the release of their first album, Aly and AJ were performing in sold-out venues as the opening act on the Cheetah-licious Christmas Tour! If you think they were nervous, you must have missed the December 2005 concert at the Orpheum Theatre in Boston, Massachusetts. "It was a good first tour," Aly says. "We definitely got some experience from that." That's a bit of understatement from Aly. Not only did she and AJ deliver an awesome set, some critics said they stole the show! Whoops, sorry, Cheetah Girls!

Aly and AJ were psyched by the reaction they received from fans. "Yeah, definitely, it's really cool," AJ told MySA.com. "When Aly's and my ears start hurting [from all the cheering], we know it's all coming together. It's pretty neat." Aly credits the sincerity of their songs with the intense fan reaction. "Our music is very inclusive," she said. "People can really listen to it and say, hey, I really know what they're singing about. I've been through that in life." In an interview with *Newsday*, she made a similar point, saying: "We want the audience to be part of the experience. After we perform the song 'Rush,' we then ask everyone to sing along with us."

It's amazing how quickly stardom can strike. Virtually overnight, Aly and AJ were being featured in magazines like *CosmoGIRL!*, *J-14*, *Twist*, *Sweet 16*, and *Tiger Beat*. That was definitely an odd feeling for the sisters. "The first time, it was, like, 'Wow, that is kind of weird,'" AJ confesses. "You don't get used to it, you get excited, but you don't tend to buy the magazines as much just because you are on it. You are more chill about it. You are, like, 'That is so cool and exciting.' The first time is when you want to soak it up because that is when it is a really big deal."

Through the spring of 2006, Aly and AJ's fan base continued to explode. To satisfy the legion of adoring listeners, a national tour was scheduled for that summer. And that's when things really took off.

Before a June 2006 concert at the Morris Performing Arts Center in South Bend, Illinois, Aly described the rush of emotions she and AJ were feeling. "It's kind of crazy to think that we wrote those songs in our bedrooms and now we're going to be performing them in front of thousands of people," she told the *South Bend Tribune*. "It's, like, 'Wow, wait a minute, rewind . . .'" Not that she was complaining, of course. "AJ and I just love performing. That's our passion."

Indeed, it's the passion that fans of Aly and AJ respond to most. Unlike a lot of so-called entertainers, who are up there onstage, lip-synching songs and going through the motions of rehearsed dance numbers, the Michalka sisters bring an inspiring freshness and energy to every performance. Even though they're naturally performers, stage fright is still part of the process. "I feel really relaxed before," Aly says. "I only get that anxious feeling in my stomach when we are standing on the sides of the stage, waiting in the wings to go on—that is when it kicks in. We are always really chill up to the point when we go up there, then AJ and I get a little bit excited. After the first song, we are off to the races and I am not nervous anymore. It is the same with AJ."

Aly and AJ may get the preconcert jitters, but their fans appreciate the authenticity of their act. Here's how one thirteen-year-old fan put it in the *South Bend Tribune*: "I think it's really cool that they write their own songs. They're different. They're not, like, you know, Britney Spears."

Everywhere Aly and AJ toured that summer, the reaction was the same. When they played the WIOG Lizard Fair in Michigan, tickets sold out in record time. "As soon as we announced the performers, parents of kids from about ten to fourteen were calling us, asking how to get tickets," Rachel Geddes, the radio station's promotion director, told the *Saginaw News*. "These are very young acts . . . but the kids who've seen them on the Disney Channel and MTV are really into them."

Later that summer, when Aly and AJ headlined at the Wilmington Flower Market in Rockford Park, Delaware, fans once again came out in droves. "From an entertainment standpoint, this is the best success we've had," Terri Pennington, chairman for the Flower Market, told the *News Journal*.

As much as the sisters were enjoying their celebrity, life on the road was definitely tough. Before rolling into Oklahoma for a performance, AJ commented in the *Tulsa World* that, "I can't even remember the last time we were in Oklahoma. Usually it's just less than twenty-four hours, and then we are off to another place. Hopefully we can stay longer this time." It was definitely a struggle for the sisters to maintain some sense of normalcy, but they did their best. "We definitely make sure we hang out with our friends," explains AJ. "We are really good about making sure we have time for normal everyday teenage things. We have a great core of friends. When you are gone, you are gone, so when you are back, you want to make sure you are with them." A night out with the Michalka sisters sounds pretty relaxed. "We love sushi, that is our favorite food, so we go out and get sushi . . . We rent movies and come home and eat chocolate chip cookie dough until we are sick. It is fun to have that in your life."

Unfortunately, as Aly and AJ got bigger, the visits home became fewer and further between. Being on tour is definitely a grind. That's one reason their mom accompanies them on the road. But even with their mom around, touring is tough on Aly and AJ. "It is so crazy," says Aly. "It is so unorganized and spontaneous and [a] fly-by-the-seat-of-your-pants lifestyle. AJ and I just roll out of bed and go to the hotel. It definitely has structure, but it is organized craziness and chaos." There are some comforts, though. "Being on the bus is really fun," Aly explains about their 2007 *Insomniatic* tour. "Hello Kitty decked out our whole bus. They are sponsoring the tour. We have pillows, blankets, a humidifier. They have a coffeepot, little Hello Kitty goblets. It is just crazy. Our bunks are decorated. They have little lights hanging. We even have dog collars and dog beds for our puppy. It is [a] nice lifestyle. It is comfortable and cozy."

The Disney people knew they had a good thing in Aly and AJ, so they did everything they could to promote the sisters. That included signing them to a multiproject deal. "Clearly, kids have connected with Alyson and Amanda, both through their TV appearances and their music, and we are thrilled to have these extraordinarily talented sisters as part of our Disney Channel family," Gary Marsh, president of entertainment at Disney Channel Worldwide, said in the *Daily News*, "As their careers continue to grow, we look forward to showcasing their talents around the world."

Once Disney put all of its weight behind Aly and AJ, their careers went from smoking to white-hot. Despite the huge success of their album, Disney wanted to continue to develop Aly's and AJ's acting careers, so they signed them on to do a pilot series called *Haversham Hall*. It is about two teenagers who were separated at childhood, only to wind up at the same prestigious boarding school. "It is a comedy drama, but it will be very mysterious and funny," Aly told *Newsday*. Though it meant even more time away from home for the sisters, they really enjoyed taping the pilot. "We had a blast shooting it," added AJ. "It is like a mystery, comedy, Nancy Drew and Harry Potter type."

The second project the girls worked on was an original television movie called *Cow Belles*. In the movie, Aly and AJ play a pair of spoiled sisters whose dad forces them to work on the family dairy farm to learn about responsibility. It's kind of like a fictionalized version of *The Simple Life*, the reality show starring Paris Hilton and Nicole Richie.

Shooting the Disney pilot and movie were definitely good experiences for Aly and AJ, but they were nothing compared with their next opportunity: starring in the made-for-TV movie production of *Super Sweet 16: The Movie*.

Based on the super-popular MTV reality show that follows spoiled kids as they plan their over-the-top, crazy lavish sweet-sixteen parties, the movie is about a couple of BFFs whose relationship is put to the test during the planning of their sixteenth birthdays. AJ landed the lead role of Sarah, lifelong friend of Jacquie, who would be played by the actress Regine Nehy. Aly, meanwhile, was perfectly cast as Taylor, an older girl at school who tries to corrupt her younger classmates with her materialism. Aly was psyched to be joining such a talented crew. "The cast was really awesome," she says. Plus, the project had so much creative appeal. "We had a lot of freedom with that, actually. That script was definitely very free. There were no restrictions like [on] the other movies I have done. This was something I could improve in and create my own character and go off. AJ and I loved that." And, of course, they liked the network! "We have MTV on all the time in our house."

Unlike the original reality show, the movie version of *Super Sweet 16* takes an unexpected moral turn as Sarah and Jacquie learn to set aside their petty concerns with things like fashion and popularity. That message really appealed to Aly and AJ, which obviously made the project even more satisfying. "It's very different because I think there's a lot more morality in the movie. I think the fact that the kids [in our movie] realize what they're doing is wrong is good," AJ told MTV.com during a break from filming. "I think that [Jacquie, like the girls on the show] forgets that this is just a party and it's not life. Real life isn't about clothes, fashion, and money. We're not gonna fly to Paris to get a dress. We're trying to show some morals. Money isn't going to get you everywhere."

As we've already seen, Aly and AJ definitely believe in causes, whether it's speaking out against bullies or raising awareness about kidnappers, so they could definitely get behind *Super Sweet 16*. Says AJ, "I think it's very cool [for celebrants] to attach themselves to a charity, to raise money and have donations at the door. It's really cool—you're having a party, but something great is coming out of it."

While Aly and AJ were filming *Super Sweet 16,* the awards kept rolling in. They won a 2005 Radio Disney Music Award for Best Song to Listen to While Getting Ready for School ("Walking on Sunshine") and Best Song from a Movie ("Rush," from another Disney made-for-TV movie, *The Twitches*.) They were nominated as Favorite Contemporary

Inspirational Artist of the Year at the American Music Awards in 2006. "Do You Believe in Magic" became the number-one requested single on Radio Disney after debuting on the Disney Channel Movie *Now You See It* (which Aly also starred in). Then, of course, there were the many public appearance, from *Good Morning America* to the lawn of the White House, where they sang "The Star Spangled Banner" on Easter Sunday.

There's no doubt about it. By the summer of 2006, Aly and AJ were bona fide superstars. But the attention wasn't going to their heads. "We are normal girls who just happen to act and sing," AJ told the *Tulsa World*. "We credit our mother for the success that we've had, and we just want to keep it going."

In fact, the only real struggle was deciding whether they wanted to pursue acting or singing. Following the Disney formula for success, they decided to do both! "I think that's what we do," Aly told the *Tulsa World*. "We go from singing to acting, and from acting to singing."

According to Aly, balancing two careers has been a challenge, but a pleasant one. "I have no idea how we juggle them," she admits. "It is wild and it is something that I can't even describe, like defying gravity. I love both. They are so different and are so special to both of us."

Obviously, their fans were hoping so as well. But celebrity stars are constantly dropping out of the scene because they can't handle the spotlight. And the spotlight was about to get blindingly bright for Aly and AJ.

CHAPTER SEVEN

Move Over, Lindsay and Hilary

The year 2005 had definitely been a good one for Aly and AJ. Their debut album had exceeded everyone's highest hopes, plus the sisters had landed numerous roles for both television and made-for-TV movies. What more could they hope for? As 2006 would prove, A LOT!

It all started with the announcement of a major, star-studded birthday bash for Radio Disney, which was being billed The Radio Disney Totally Birthday 10 Concert. The date was set for July 22, at Arrowhead Pond arena in Anaheim, California. In planning the concert lineup, the bigwigs at Disney thought long and hard about which performers best represented the company over the past decade. It would be like an all-star team of Disney talent, with each performer getting fifteen minutes onstage to remind everyone why they were on top. Names like Jesse McCartney, Miley Cyrus, and The Cheetah Girls were automatic picks, and, much to their surprise and delight, so were Aly and AJ! It's pretty amazing that just one year into their careers, the Michalka sisters were already being linked with the industry's most established acts. "It was definitely an honor," admits Aly. "That was a huge deal for us and a huge celebration. We were with a lot of Disney Channel stars that were there to support the station. We were very excited."

Buzz surrounding the concert quickly reached a deafening level. Tickets were sold out in no time flat, and scalpers were charging $129 on the Internet for a single seat! Disney wasn't kidding when it called the concert the single biggest event in the history of the company. And there were Aly and AJ, the golden-coiffed darlings of the evening! Their fifteen-minute set was considered one of the most showstopping by many fans in the crowd, and others who tuned in to view the live webcast. One reviewer went so far as to write: "Move over, Lindsay and Hilary. Here come Aly and AJ. The sister act is the latest teen sensation to break out of Hollywood."

It's hard to block out those kinds of comments, but the ever-modest Michalka girls never got caught up in the popularity contests. "I don't mind [the comparisons]. AJ and I definitely have our own voice and our own sound, so it is hard to compare. When people ask us what we think our music is like, it's, like, 'Aly and AJ.' It is a compliment when people compare us to other acts that are successful. If we can be that successful and remembered like that, than we are doing good."

As it turned out, the comparisons would get harder to avoid. That's because the Disney Anniversary Tour was just one celebrity collaboration that Aly and AJ would take part in that summer. In August 2006, they were included on the release of the *Girl Next* album, along with the likes of Kelly Clarkson and Vanessa Hudgens. A few months later, Aly and AJ popped up on another compilation album called *Radio Disney Party Jams*, which featured Hilary Duff and the cast of *High School Musical*.

The Michalkas were also busy in the summer of 2006 making the deluxe edition of *Into the Rush*, which included three new tracks, among them the smash hit "Chemicals React." Once they put the finishing touches on the deluxe edition, they launched right into the recording of a holiday album, which they decided to call *Acoustic Hearts of Winter*.

The funny thing about that experience was that in order to get the album into stores by Christmas, they had to record it during the dog days of summer! Of course, the sisters took it in stride, with a little help from their team. "Our producers, Tim James and Antonina Armato, wanted to make sure we got in the spirit, so they filled the studio with Christmas decorations, even Christmas cookies and a tree with gifts we can open when we're done," Aly told the *Saginaw News*. There are a few perks to Christmas in summer!

Not surprisingly, the always-professional Michalka girls finished the Christmas album right on schedule. It ended up being a combination of cover songs, including classics like "Silent Night" and "Joy to the World," and original recordings, such as "Greatest Time of the Year" and "Not This Year." *Acoustic Hearts of Winter* hit the shelves on September 26, 2006, and received the same lavish praise given to *Into the Rush*. In the end, it became the second best-selling holiday album of 2006. Again, fans and critics respected Aly and AJ's musical prowess, as well as the themes of generosity and empowerment that their songwriting taps into. Those themes were especially prevalent on the spiritual-based Christmas album, which goes from rollicking to heartfelt.

"It's a project that has a special connection for us because of what we believe in," Aly told the *Saginaw News*. "We're honored to have the chance."

Between the success of their second album and the live performances they continued to give, Aly and AJ were getting hotter and hotter. Even when it was clear that their success was no fluke, the sisters had trouble believing their luck. "We're blown away by how well we've done," AJ told the *Home News Tribune*, though at the same time, they didn't feel like it had been handed to them for free. "Everything is great, but we've worked so hard for it, which is fine," AJ continued. "We love what we do. A lot of people just think that it's an easy world we're in. We make music and we act, but it's very demanding. We wouldn't do this if we didn't love it."

With fame comes responsibility, as more and more people started to look to Aly and AJ as role models. Fortunately, the sisters were up for the challenge. "It is good to be a role model," says Aly. "There is [a] certain standard that you have to uphold and I don't mind having that kind of pressure. AJ and I want to be role models and to inspire kids and older people as well. We want to grow as artists. We want to grow up, but not grow out. I think that is something that you have to be careful of it as an artist . . . It is important not to alienate the fans."

Of course, Aly and AJ were fortunate to have two pretty fantastic role models of their own in their mother and father. "They have been really great on the support they have given us and raising us like normal kids. Even though we are in a crazy business, we are not like business children. That is all because of our parents. They have been really great role models and taught us to stay really grounded. They are always there no matter what . . . Our mom has never missed one of our shows.

Being such positive role models really endeared Aly and AJ to a lot of companies. As 2006 slipped into 2007, the sisters were chosen to represent several products. There was the Post Honeycomb Cereal content that they were the face of, as well as the Aly and AJ line of merchandising that was being introduced at Target stores. They even found themselves attached to The Sims, the super-popular EA video game, when their hit single "Chemicals React" was translated into Simlish.

Believe it or not, the sisters were super-excited! "We are HUGE fans of The Sims, so it was really cool to be tapped to provide music for their latest project, The Sims 2 Pets," AJ said in *Business Wire*. "When we told EA that we could speak Simlish they were really psyched! It was fun to reinterpret our song for The Sims and ultimately, our fans." It's actually not surprising that Aly and AJ like The Sims so much, given the parallels between the game and their music. As Aly explained: "One of the things I have always liked about the The Sims games is that they are very inclusive, people can play out real storylines from their lives—like a romantic relationship that's really gotten stressful—and there isn't a lot of judgment. We try to do the same thing with our music, give people something that they can relate to, so they think, 'I really get that, I've been through it!'"

With all the promotional work Aly and AJ were doing, it was hard to find time to do what they love the most: make music. But eventually they found a way to balance their busy schedule so that they could work on their third album. The release date for the album, which was given the name *Insomniatic*, was set for July 2007.

The best artists—whether they're musicians, painters, or architects—are constantly testing the limits of their creativity. It's how they keep their edge, and Aly and AJ would be no different. "You can categorize our music as pop with a whole lot of melody in it, but on the next album we want to have a little more rock and try to mix things up," AJ told the *Tulsa World*. "It's all about reinventing yourself, because if you don't, you won't be around very long."

The album kept the Michalkas busy for most of the spring, though they of course had time to celebrate their birthdays. Aly turned eighteen on March 25 and AJ turned sixteen on April 10, though the big party didn't happen until May 14. But if you happen to have been there that night at Les Deux Café, the red-hot Hollywood nightclub, you know it was worth the wait. "We rented out this club and invited tons of friends, like three hundred people," recalls AJ. "We rolled in on eighteen huge motorcycle choppers and [we had a] red carpet and paparazzi and our logo was everywhere. We had, like, two wardrobe changes. It was completely dramatic and fun.

Inside, the sisters were greeted by a group of close friends, including Miley Cyrus, Emma Roberts (niece of Julia), and Zelda Williams (daughter of Robin). Not that it was a celebrities-only affair. "We still have friends that aren't in the business, too," AJ says. "But I feel like it is easier when we have friends in the business only because they really know what you are going through because they are going through the same thing. I feel bad when people who aren't in the business, are like, 'Dude where are you? Why haven't you called me?' I'm, like, 'I'm sorry. I am so busy.' They don't really understand as much. But we definitely still have friends that aren't in the business."

The gang whooped it up all night long, dancing to their favorite music, including a live half-hour set by the Plain White T's, and, yes, flirting innocently with some of the cute guys on hand. It all ended innocently enough (though not early!). "We were up to five a.m. partying and dancing and hanging with our friends," remembers Aly. "We actually went back to the hotel and just kind of chilled and got into our pajamas and had a couple friends over that were really close to us."

Obviously, the A-list celebrity set was taking a shine to Aly and AJ. In fact, this acceptance led to one of the sister's funniest TV acting appearances of all time. Well, actually only AJ was acting. It was for the show *Punk'd*, in which superhot Ashton Kutcher plays practical jokes on his friends in Hollywood. In this episode, he enlists AJ to help make her sister think that she's poisoned an enormous bear during a photo shoot. If you haven't seen it yet, run—don't walk—to the nearest computer and download the clip. The expression on Aly's face is hilarious!

Getting picked to appear on *Punk'd* is definitely one of those unwritten signs that you've arrived—not that Aly and AJ needed much convincing by that point. They had definitely made it to the A-list. There's a lot of glitter and glam, but there's also tons of pressure. Many stars crack under it. The big question now was, would Aly and AJ?

CHAPTER EIGHT

Keepin' the Faith

The Michalka household that Aly and AJ grew up in was firmly rooted in religious faith. The morals, guidelines, beliefs, and strength that the sisters learned from their parents have infiltrated every aspect of every day of their lives, not just on Sundays when they are sitting in church.

Their high ideals have kept them from getting carried away by their insane success as pop stars. While many musicians quickly lose sight of their true friends and the hard work ethic that got them into the spotlight in the first place, Aly and AJ are constantly reminded that they are just a tiny part of a very big universe. Now that's humbling! They understand there are many things in life way more important than their fame. "We're all about staying grounded," Aly told ChristianityToday.com. "Our parents have been great, letting AJ and I know where they stand, and we're definitely remembering God is way bigger than all of this. It was cool to be able to do this, yet realize it's not your whole life. There's a lot more than acting and singing, even though we love it."

Their belief in God hasn't just kept them grounded, it's also been a big force in shaping them as musicians. Attending church and listening to Christian music forms the backbone of their career. Their mom, Carrie, has inspired the girls musically from the get-go and she was the lead singer in a Christian group called The J.C. Band. And, of course, one of the very first places the sisters started singing in public was in their church. These are formative experiences for the girls, and not ones they could easily leave behind as they grew up.

When Aly and AJ tackle the issues of spirituality and belief in their songs, many music lovers are excited to hear these themes put to very cool tunes. It's certainly a break from a lot of the same stuff about parties, cars, and hooking up that you get in pop music. For many people, Aly and AJ put out messages they could really relate to. "It's been really positive and cool," AJ told ChristianityToday.com. "Some fans have mentioned that they love the music and can relate because they're believers too, which is just huge."

So it's no surprise that Aly and AJ would be big on the Christian rock scene, a genre that has grown significantly over the years as producers and promoters have come to understand that rock and religion can actually mix. If you're not familiar with Christian rock, put away those images of a guy playing an accordion in a church basement somewhere. The contemporary Christian music industry witnessed an explosion of Christian rock bands coming on the scene in the 1990s. The movement continues today with everything from Christian punk to hip-hop to metal to ska. It seems no genre is off-limits to Christian musicians. There are even Christian Goth bands!

For Aly and AJ, the Christian connection to their music is purely a personal one. "When we write songs they come from an emotional place that's direct from our hearts," AJ told ChristianityToday.com. "They're vulnerable. A lot of our songs have [spiritual inspiration] behind them, even if it's not specifically worshipping God or Jesus." The only song they have released on Christian rock radio is "Never Far Behind," which shot to number one on the Christian charts. The song has a lot of universal messages. For instance, with these lyrics, it discourages giving in to peer pressure:

I know this really isn't you
I know your heart is somewhere else
And I'll do anything I can
To help you break out of this spell

It isn't a harsh, fire-and-brimstone kind of tune, but one that offers forgiveness. "There is always room for change," the lyrics say. "You're allowed to make mistakes. It's a part of every life."

"Never Far Behind" might have been a hit single on Christian charts, but don't call the Michalka sisters Christian rockers. Although their music definitely comes from that perspective, Aly and AJ insist they don't make music for Christians alone. The sisters don't like being labeled Christian artists, because they hope their music appeals to a much wider group of people than those from just one faith. "We don't ever wanna preach or shove anything down people's throats," Aly told *Blender*. "AJ and I want our music to be inspiring . . . We don't want to exclude anybody." AJ backed her sister up: "If we have a Muslim fan or an atheist fan, that's their thing—I'm gonna love them no matter what."

You don't have to go to a synagogue, mosque, or church to get their music. You can still be impressed that they are speaking up for their beliefs, even if you don't share the same ones. Or, as AJ put it, "People also appreciate that we express our beliefs through music."

One of Aly and AJ's major beliefs is that with great reward comes great responsibility. That means because they have been blessed with fame and fortune, they need to put their blessings to good use. Celebrities today have so much power and status in our society. Many people look to them as role models. But lots of stars don't want to or can't handle that responsibility. Look at all the actors, models, musicians, and athletes who prefer to use their fame to get into clubs every night rather than set a better example of living. Or how about those who purposefully engage in outlandish behavior to draw attention to themselves? We're not naming names, but we've seen them plastered all over the tabloids for such tricks.

But Aly and AJ are celebrities of a different breed. They're thrilled to be role models and work hard to maintain that coveted position. "I think it's awesome," Aly told the *San Antonio Express-News* about setting a good example for kids. "It's funny because a lot of people will say, 'Oh no, I never got into this business to be a role model.' But I think you have to accept that. I think it's good to have responsibility and hold yourself accountable."

That's a message parents can get behind. In fact, parents like almost everything about Aly and AJ's music, which is a good thing since they hear a lot of it in the car, at home, wherever. Not only are the tunes catchy, but also the lyrics don't contain any language objectionable to parents. Aly and AJ offer a nice alternative to the parade of current pop stars shaking their things in skimpy clothes. "If you have children aged seven to thirteen, especially girls, there seems to be no escape [from Aly and AJ's music]," Dana Willhoit wrote for *The Ledger*. "But if you listen to a few Aly and AJ songs, I think you'll find this isn't such a bad thing." Dana's point is proven at the live concerts where moms and dads can be found rocking out right next to their kids, which is just fine with Aly and AJ. "That's really cool because parents come and listen, and they enjoy it," Aly told the *San Antonio Express-News*. "They come up to us and say, 'Wow, thank you for making great music that my kids can listen to.'"

Being a high-profile role model extends past music with uplifting lyrics and into everyday life. Because AJ and Aly are so famous, there is a lot of scrutiny when it comes to their personal lives. Some stars resent this kind of attention, but again, the sisters understand that they are in a privileged position and are ready for the challenge. If they were to go out and get drunk or do drugs, kids who look up to them might get the wrong idea "I understand how some people have certain ideas and thoughts and that their personal lives are none of the public's business," Aly told ChristianityToday.com. "But if I put myself in a situation where I'm seen by millions of kids, I have some sort of responsibility, no matter what. There's no excuse to [behave poorly], because people are looking up to you. That just comes with the territory."

You see, celebrity isn't all gifts, suites, and award ceremonies. Giving back has become as important a part of stardom as walking the red carpet. Many celebs pick a pet charity and either offer money, time, or simply their famous name to the cause. Angelina Jolie is the supreme example of this. As a Goodwill Ambassador for the United Nations, Angelina has worked tirelessly on behalf of the twenty million refugees around the world. She has used her glamour and the interest in her personal life to highlight the plight of those much less fortunate. She's only one example. There are plenty more examples—such as actor Michael J. Fox's Foundation for Parkinson's Research, or Paul Newman, who donates all the profits from Newman's Own products to charity.

This is one trend Aly and AJ are happy to follow. The sisters have lent their star power to the AmberWatch Foundation, which is dedicated to the prevention of child abduction. The Foundation's website states that its mission by the end of 2008 is "to educate 25 million elementary-aged children, and their parents" on how to stay out of dangerous situations. As co-chairpersons for the Children's Advisory Board of the AmberWatch Foundation, Aly and AJ have championed this mission. "AmberWatch came to us after hearing our song," Aly explains. "They somehow got a hold of it and said, 'Wow, you guys would be great spokespeople for our Foundation.' AJ and I were so excited to hear that they wanted to team up with us. We do a lot of charity work with them and being able to get the Foundation out there and let people know about some really good safety tips. It's really cool. We are definitely donating money towards preventing child kidnapping." With Teri Hatcher as the Foundation's National Spokesperson, Aly and AJ are in very good company.

Despite their passion for AmberWatch, Aly and AJ couldn't pick just one charity. The young musicians also served as the official spokespeople for Samsung's 2007 Hope for Education program, which was created by the electronics company to lessen the technology gap in the educational system. With a little help from Microsoft, the program has forked over more than $2 million in hardware and software to K–12 schools throughout the country that submitted essays for a competition detailing how technology helps kids learn. Samsung chose Aly and AJ to kick off Hope for Education's fourth year with a special concert April 11. Samsung president and CEO D. J. Oh explained that out of all the celebrities in the world, the electronics company chose Aly and AJ because, "These young women will help Samsung communicate directly to their young fans, many of which attend schools that lack the funding to purchase the kind of technology necessary to keep them competitive with the rest of the world."

When Aly and AJ join a cause, it's not just lip service. So they didn't just play a concert to publicize this cause, they also read through the students' essays and helped a council made up of academics decide the winning entries. "Receiving the best education possible has been very important to us," the girls said in a statement at the time of the contest. "We encourage all of our fans who want to help better their schools' technological resources to enter the essay contest."

Aly and AJ have received so much encouragement from their family, friends, fans, and each other that they have plenty to share with others.

That Aly and AJ share the same faith is a big part of their chemistry, but it's nothing compared to the fact that they share the same last name. Sisterhood is definitely what defines the Michalka girls!

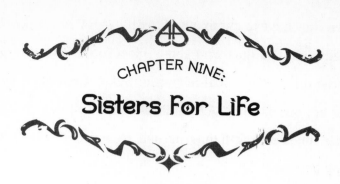

CHAPTER NINE

Sisters For Life

Sibling relationships are the most important bonds for a lot of people. After all, sisters and brothers are there from the very beginning, unlike best friends, who may not arrive on the scene until elementary school or later. As a result, people learn a lot about life (and themselves) through their interactions with their siblings.

Because Aly and AJ were born so close together, they experienced even more of the world around them through similar eyes. So much so that it's actually sometimes hard to tell which one of them is the older sister in the relationship—even for Aly and AJ! "I think we were born out of order," Aly confided in *Tiger Beat* magazine. "She's very much like the older sister I look up to."

Of course, there are plenty of times when Aly steps up to the part of big sister—for instance, every morning when they have to climb out of bed! When the *Sun-Sentinel* asked the Michalkas who gets up last in the morning, Aly offered this unequivocal response: "AJ, definitely. I have to drag her out of bed!" AJ didn't put up much of a defense, citing her sleeping habits as one reason she has "really crazy bed head."

Aly may have trouble pulling her kid sister out of bed each day, but once the two are up, they're very much together. They're constantly referring to each other as their best friend, and if you've ever seen them in public, you know they're not just saying that. The girls truly respect the bond of sisterhood. It's not surprising that one of the greatest musical influences in their lives is the band Heart, led by siblings Ann and Nancy Wilson. "They're sisters and amazing songwriters, and they've accomplished so much," Aly told the *Lexington Herald-Leader*. "We really look up to them."

Even with entertainers closer to them in age, Aly and AJ are constantly seeking out sister acts to admire. There's definitely a long tradition of hardworking and, as a result, hugely successful, sisters throughout history. Type "famous sisters" into Wikipedia.com and you get over forty names from all walks of life. There's Venus and Serena Williams, stars of the tennis circuit, who have racked up more Grand Slam titles than any other set of siblings; Charlotte, Emily, and Anne Brontë, sensations of the nineteenth-century literary world (if you haven't come across them in English class yet, don't worry, you will!); and tons of sisters from the modern-day entertainment industry, including Britney and Jamie Lynn Spears, Jessica and Ashlee Simpson, Paris and Nicky Hilton, and Lindsay and Aliana Lohan.

These sisters have all been made stronger by their sibling relationships, but it's doubtful that they've been as intimate as Aly and AJ. Closely listening to their lyrics (which of course they write together) shows the depth of their relationship. Consider the opening lyrics to the song "On the Ride," from their debut album *Into the Rush*:

> We don't have to try
> To think the same thoughts
> We just have a way
> OF knowin' everything's gonna be OK

The song is obviously all about their sisterhood. In it, Aly and AJ seem to be saying that they're so close, they don't constantly need to be "working" on their relationship. The love, respect, and affection just come naturally. "We are very different people, but we are also very much alike," says AJ. "We might have different tastes in certain things but when it comes down to it, we end up agreeing on the same thing, which is pretty bizarre. We read each other's minds every day . . . We will look at each other and will know exactly what the other person is thinking. The connection we have is different. We know a lot of siblings and they are really close, but there is something that Aly and I have. I think it is because we work together and are best friends. That is what makes it different. We work together, but we don't get sick of each other. We really are best friends."

Of course, Aly and AJ are human beings, so they do have the occasional tiff. "It is a very exciting roller coaster that AJ and I are on," explains Aly. "There are ups and downs. We have our moments where we disagree and will fight, but at the end of the day, we love each other. We are so close. We don't forget who we are as people, and can check in and say, 'Hey dude, stop acting like a weirdo.' We are there for each other, and that is going to help us stay grounded and normal and not get caught up in the crazy Hollywood crowd."

Aly and AJ are definitely each talented in their own rights. That's why they've been able to emerge as huge stars, both in their solo careers and as a sister act. As Aly explained in the *Lexington Herald-Leader*, when asked how their relationship will shape their careers, "Music is always going to be, at least for a while, something that we do together. On the acting side, there are going to be projects we want to do on our own."

Most sibling duos follow a similar path. They will work together for a long stretch of time and then break apart periodically to pursue separate passions. At this stage in their lives, it's hard to say how long Aly and AJ will be best known throughout the industry as the Michalka sisters. "I don't see us ever doing music alone," says AJ. "It is something different when we get onstage together or get in the vocal booth together. That is when it is really magical. I feel there is this chemistry when the both of us are singing. It is better when it is the both of us." Even if they start putting out solo albums one day and starring in separate movies, they're always going to be two of the closest sisters in all of entertainment.

CHAPTER TEN:
Extraordinary Girls, Regular Lives

Aly and AJ have been all over the country performing in front of thousands of screaming fans. They have graced magazine covers and made highly produced music videos. They have starred in TV shows and made-for-TV movies. They wear the latest fashions to their birthday parties with super A-list guests at exclusive clubs, and they get to meet their celebrity crushes in the flesh.

This doesn't sound like the lives of two girls who still live at home. But that's exactly where Aly and AJ reside. Sure, they could buy a place of their own. They could buy houses for everyone in their family and fill them with the hippest furnishings available. They could have a slick loft somewhere downtown where they blast music at top volume until all hours of the night. Still, they prefer to stick to their parents' rules, keeping things cozy with dear old

Mom and Dad. That's why the Michalkas all live together in a gated community in Calabasas, California. The exclusive neighborhood provides security, which is really important because of the sisters' skyrocketing fame. They aren't the only celebs seeking anonymity within the confines of these fancy culs-de-sac. Travis Barker—drummer for the band Blink-182 and star of the MTV reality show *Meet the Barkers*, which gave a glimpse into his life with then-wife, former Miss USA, Shanna Moakler—lives in the same development as the Michalkas. And the house where Nick Lachey and Jessica Simpson lived when they were married and had their own MTV reality show is just one development over.

Despite their famous neighbors, some of whom sport Mohawks and tons of tattoos à la Travis Barker, the Michalka household isn't different from many homes across the country. Ok, it is a multimillion-dollar mansion, but the spirit's the same. And AJ's bedroom couldn't be more classic girlie teen if she had a set designer dress it. Yet the room is sophisticated, too. "It recently got painted a rich brown," says AJ. "It is beautiful. My whole room is really peaceful. It is very French. It is a nice sanctuary to come home to after we come back from set. I have a balcony off my room and I hang out there at night when it is really warm. I have this great bathroom and a walk-in closet. Our whole house is decorated really beautifully. We always have tons of candles, like hundreds of candles, it's insane. My family is obsessed with candles."

As for Aly's room, it evokes a similar feeling. "It is very moody," she says. "I am romantic, and it is kind of dark. It is kind of vintage-y and very eclectic. It has a lot of cranberry. I like hanging fairies in my room. My pillows have black lace. It is kind of gothic. It is very relaxing. I have a bunch of candles and my books stacked up. I have this cool mannequin that has this really neat dress on it that AJ got it. I have my own fashion wall."

Like ordinary American kids, Aly and AJ have pets they adore. Both serious animal lovers, they grew up with two dogs named Toby and Saint, and they can often be found frolicking with their new pets. Says Aly: "We have two puppies, Roadie and Willow, and Bandit [their older dog]. The new puppies are called Teddy Bears. They are a mix between a bichon [frise] and shih tzu. Mine is Roadie, and AJ's is Willow."

They like to play with their dogs and have their childhood bedrooms intact in their parents' home, but what about the wild parties and the crazy club hopping that all celebrities are supposed to engage in these days? That's one perk of being famous that Aly and AJ are happy to forgo. "It's tiresome to go out to parties, fake your way through them and pretend you're having a good time," Aly told *Blender*.

For the sisters, the ideal night has nothing to do with popular restaurants like Nobu or Mr. Chow. And they are far away from nightclubs and velvet ropes. They love nothing more than to kick back and spend a totally normal night at home.

So what's on the agenda for these two famous homebodies during a typical laid-back evening in the Michalka house? Well, there's definitely a movie. Aly and AJ both say that *Willow* is one of their favorite films of all time. The 1988 fantasy flick, directed by Ron Howard, is a classic. Based on a story by *Star Wars* director George Lucas, the tale centers around a farmer named Willow, who is part of a magical group of people called Nelwyns. He's compelled to leave his home in order to save a baby girl from an evil queen. Along the way, he has plenty of adventures. Aly has other film faves—a bona fide Johnny Depp and Jack Black freak, she is perfectly content to watch *The School of Rock* or *Pirates of the Caribbean* any day.

Aly and AJ don't have much downtime with their busy work schedules, but when they do, the sisters like to veg out in front of the television. AJ and Aly are both addicted to *That '70s Show*, a sitcom that originally aired on Fox. The show, which is now in reruns, stars the adorable Topher Grace. It also gave young actors Mila Kunis, Laura Prepon, Wilmer Valderrama, and Danny Masterson their start. Not to mention catapulting Ashton Kutcher, who played the lovably dumb character Michael Kelso, to the top of the Hollywood A-list. Aly's other guilty TV pleasures include reruns of *The O.C.*, starring the very fashionable Mischa Barton, and pretty much anything on MTV. She has to check out the competition, right?

The sisters also really like a good book. "We read a lot, all the time," Aly says. "We go to Barnes and Noble. That is our favorite place. The only bummer is that I'll go in there and will get stopped and all I want to do is find a book. I tend to read fantasy and comedy and drama books, teen books, coming-of-age stories, I like that kind of stuff. Some action-mystery stuff too." One of their favorite book series is Lemony Snicket's A *Series of Unfortunate Events*. The first of the thirteen books, written by Daniel Handler under the pseudonym Lemony Snicket and illustrated by Brett Helquist, is *The Bad Beginning*. You can get an idea of the book's tone just from its title. The series follows three unlucky siblings—Violet, Klaus, and Sunny Baudelaire—after their parents have died in a fire. Dark humor and cynical commentary fills the pages as the orphans go through adventure after adventure. Aly and AJ probably find the books a refreshing change from their singularly charmed lives.

Aly and AJ certainly have a superactive side. When they aren't on tour and rocking out in front of thousands, they have tons of energy that they love to burn off by horseback riding or mountain biking. It's a great relief from the hours and hours they spend sitting cooped up on a tour bus with nothing to do. Aly enjoys a wide range of sports that include volleyball, swimming, and rock climbing. She is a total adrenaline junkie. She told the Fort Lauderdale *Sun-Sentinel* that if she could have one superpower, "I would want to fly. I love the feeling of being on a roller coaster or being in a car with the top down. I think that would be really rad."

AJ doesn't need the great outdoors or a huge animal to let off a little steam. She will think nothing of dancing around (another one of her favorite activities) wherever she can. It doesn't take much more than some good tunes and she starts going nuts. One time, AJ went so crazy dancing in her room that she injured herself! "I spun around and my toe went underneath my foot and I broke my toe!" she said. "They don't have toe casts, so they had to put on a big padded cast instead. It went up to my knee!" AJ is so cool, she doesn't mind being a dork sometimes.

Although the sisters live at home, relish quiet nights in front of the television, and do sports during their free time, that's basically where their typical teen status ends. Of course, being on the road touring with their albums or shooting on location make their lives extraordinary. And it has impacted their education. Aly and AJ are both all finished with school, but when they were students, they attended an independent study charter school that allowed them to do their work on the road but still take tests in a normal classroom environment. It also meant the girls got finished with school much more quickly since they took classes year-round. Aly doesn't feel bad about having missed out on the typical high school experience—big classrooms filled with rowdy kids; noisy cafeterias; and lots of competition. "We're definitely not the normal teens, going to the high school dance," Aly admitted to the *Saginaw News*. "It's worth it in my eyes, and it's by choice."

That doesn't mean that Aly and AJ didn't get a stellar education. It was just different from that of the average American teen. Aly found plenty to praise about the way she and her sister went to school. "[I] love the one-on-one with a teacher," she told ChristianityToday.com. "It's interesting to see how we can study and maintain friendships, but somehow it all works out for us." Aly graduated as the valedictorian of her class in 2006 and AJ followed as her class's valedictorian in 2007, but both sisters walked together in AJ's ceremony. Aly had missed her own graduation because she was rocking out at a concert in New York City.

Both Aly and AJ hope to attend college one day. "Definitely," Aly told the Fort Lauderdale *Sun-Sentinel*. "It probably won't be at the same time other people would go . . . not at the same age, but it's definitely something I want to do." AJ agreed wholeheartedly, adding that she thinks it "would be a really neat experience and I'd love to go somewhere in state, in California, like Pepperdine." Wherever the sisters end up, they are sure to be a success.

What about love? Celebrity doesn't just make studying

hard. Believe it or not, it also makes dating kind of difficult. Sure, if you're a star, you can have your hair and makeup done and look great. But it makes meeting a normal guy who likes you just for you and not all your celebrity trappings a real challenge. Often stars will go out with other stars. It's only natural that people gravitate to others with whom they can share all aspects of their lives. If Aly or AJ were to go out with another musician or actor, that guy wouldn't be freaked out by walking a red carpet or having fans clamor for his girlfriend's autograph. The girls keep news of their love life pretty quiet. "I think that it's really important to keep your personal life private," Aly told the *Toronto Sun*.

Between romance, rock 'n' roll, and all their other activities, it's a wonder Aly and AJ don't collapse from exhaustion. In order to keep their energy level up, they find moments for rejuvenation even in a packed schedule. "We love going to the spa," Aly told *Newsday*. "That is such a big deal for us because we have such limited time. It is just great to go there, get away from the world, and just be ourselves."

Both sisters also try to keep things healthy when it comes to eating. As popular celebrities, their image is extremely important, so they have to maintain their slim figures. But they can't starve themselves or else they wouldn't be able to rock the arena crowds every night. The answer is a menu packed with fresh fruits and veggies. While AJ loves to whip up a great meal, Aly sometimes just can't resist junk food. She loves to indulge in salty snacks like tacos, and sugary treats such as Ring Pops and Pop Rocks. But she balances it out with healthier options such as sushi. It's hard to eat right when they are out on the road, so AJ and Aly are known to get their vitamins by downing shots of wheatgrass and their favorite healthy Jamba Juice smoothies such as Razzmatazz or Banana Berry. It might not be a home-cooked meal, but it's better than Pop Rocks!

No matter how busy AJ and Aly get, they always make time to keep in touch with their old friends and to hang out with them whenever time permits. Seeing friendly faces, from a time before the sisters turned into superstars, is an important tool in keeping their lives real. "We have friends from church, school, [along with] songwriters and actors," Aly told *Newsday*. "They are all very cool and supportive. They still know us as the same Aly and AJ as the ones they used to play Barbie dolls with."

Maintaining a down-to-earth attitude is of supreme importance to Aly and AJ. They come in contact with so many stars whose big egos have turned their success sour. The sisters aren't afraid of that happening to them. "I could see how this could happen to some, maybe those who weren't raised with the morals we have, but we've been brought up in a home where we can't get away with that stuff," Aly told ChristianityToday.com. "We're not better than anybody, and we're all equal at the foot of the cross. We've been brought up like that and are not bent toward going off the deep end."

With that attitude, the sisters certainly have a bright future ahead of them. So what are their goals in the years to come? Aly and AJ aren't looking to conquer the world. They want always to be themselves and have fun doing just that. Aly summed up their life philosophy to the *Toronto Sun*, which is to "just love what you're doing and enjoy it and take every moment that comes your way."

So whether the sisters are topping the music charts or simply picking out tunes on guitars in the living room at home, you know they'll be making music. "If we don't book the next movie, or [if] we stop selling CDs, we're not gonna freak out and crawl into a hole," AJ told *Blender.* "It's a true passion. We'd still be doing it, professionally or not. On MTV or in our rooms." Now that's dedication.

CHAPTER ELEVEN

What's Next?

Aly and AJ have already been on hit TV shows, starred in original TV movies, released albums, and toured all over the country—and they are still teenagers! So what's next for this dynamic duo? Plenty!

On July 10, 2007, *Insomniatic*, Aly and AJ's newest album, dropped into stores across the country, and it is garnering high praise from critics and fans alike. The word "insomniatic" was coined by Aly and AJ and they define it as "the state of mind where one becomes addicted to the deprivation of sleep caused by an epic revelation of joy." Aly and AJ have plenty to be joyful about. The girls kicked off a forty-city tour immediately after the album's release. *Teen People* put *Insomniatic* on its "Summer's Hottest New Music" List. And *Billboard*'s reviewer gushed, ". . . the teen princesses of Radio Disney and their own branding empire construct an endlessly ambitious yet endlessly effervescent confessional pop-rock breakup album that deserves to carry them far beyond their teen pop base . . . Departures range from the delirious '80s California new wave amusement-park pop of 'Like Whoa' to the title cut's blurry-eyed Nirvana pastiche to 'Bullseye,' with power chords hitting the spot like its title. Tunes are dressed up in a heavenly Europop-synth sparkle, and the lyrics—frequently harmonized through complex Destiny's Child time signatures—turn blood on the tracks into a celebration." The album hit number 15 on the *Billboard* charts, and its first single, "Potential Breakup Song," was already number 17 on the Billboard Hot 100 chart after only two weeks! "Potential Breakup Song" was also the sixth most downloaded single overall on iTunes during the debut week of *Insomniatic*. Way to go, Aly and AJ!

The girls are also ready to grace the silver screen. Aly and AJ have both been auditioning for roles, and it won't be long before it pays off. In fact, AJ starts filming *The Lovely Bones* alongside Ryan Gosling and Rachel Weisz in late 2007. The film is based on the 2002 best-selling novel by Alice Sebold and will be directed by Peter Jackson, who also directed the big-budget *Lord of the Rings* trilogy. *The Lovely*

Bones is the story of a young girl who is brutally murdered and watches from heaven as her family is affected by her death. It's a chillingly sad story, but you can count on AJ to do it justice.

One thing is certain: No matter what Aly and AJ decide to do next, you can be sure it will be a success!

CHAPTER TWELVE

Sister Style Guide

No matter how much they are photographed or how many tour dates they book, Aly and AJ never seem to ever have a bad fashion day. You know, the kind where your socks don't really match your shorts. Or your shirt's riding up to reveal hand-me-down high-waisted jeans. Sure, they have the big bucks to spend on whatever outfits their heart desires, but that's not the secret to their style success. Here are a few simple rules that keep Aly and AJ looking good.

It's okay to get a little fashion advice:

Aly and AJ have a strong sense of personal style and are fearless shoppers who brave the high-end, super-chic shops in SoHo whenever they visit New York City on tour. But that doesn't mean they are above getting expert help when it comes to how they look. They often consult a stylist.

That's a person with amazing fashion sense, who is paid to put together outfits. Pretty cool job, right? It can mean anything from shopping for a client to borrowing items (such as expensive jewels), to rifling through the person's closet to put together a supremely great look. Aly and AJ, of course, share a stylist. Why wouldn't they, since they share practically everything else? Their go-to fashion team is Paula Bradley and Matt Goldman or Tara Swennen. Aly and AJ work closely with their stylists to make sure they are still expressing their true selves through their clothes. Tara dressed the girls for their birthday bash and for the American Music Awards. Paula and Matt dress them for their music videos and tours. They also dress the gorgeous and super-funky singer Kelis. Paula described her personal fashion philosophy to *Beauty Business* this way: "My style is definitely mine. Fashion-forward, but more woman than girl. Always a touch of rock 'n' roll elegance. No respect for trend authority." Rock 'n' roll elegance? No wonder Aly and AJ hired Paula. That phrase describes the sisters to a tee.

Tip: Okay, so you can't afford a stylist on your allowance. That doesn't mean you have to brave the shopping mall, or your closet, alone. If your wardrobe is filled with tons of things you don't wear anymore, encourage an older sister or a really trustworthy friend to help you through the process of "editing," as stylists call it. That's where you try on all questionable clothes and your "stylist" gives it the honest thumbs-up or down (the thumbs-down pile heads straight to Goodwill). Another fun idea is to go shopping with a friend and choose outfits for each other to try on. You may just expand your style in all the right ways.

Experimenting is good, when it comes to clothes:

Having a sense of style doesn't mean wearing a uniform. We're all familiar with the legions of girls strolling into school with matching low-rise jeans, baby-doll tops, and pointy shoes—or whatever the trend du jour is. Aly and AJ aren't afraid to mix things up a little when it comes to their outfits. "Our look? We love to change it up," Aly told the *San Antonio Express-News*. "We don't ever want to be, like, boring. Our look is very casual, but approachable still." Aly is all about experimenting with fashion. "I will try anything on," she admits. "I like to wear aprons over my jeans. I always wear these black rubber bracelets. I tie my laces different ways.

I always like black laces. I like to experiment with different things. I'm into mixing vintage with modern." She also loves to sew her own creations, and she also takes old clothes and rips them up to make something new. Inspired by other rock-stars-turned-fashion-designers like Gwen Stefani, Aly hopes to start her own designer clothing line!

Tip: Break out of the mold, in little ways or big. Shake up your usual routine by pairing jeans with something bolder than a T-shirt. Try a flowing minidress over a pair of straight or skinny leg jeans. Or take one of your mom's scarves (with her permission, of course!) and tie it around your head to channel some Jennifer Lopez glamour. There are countless ways to push your style, so find the way that's right for you. Who knows? Soon you may be ripping up and creating your own clothes!

Don't be afraid to be neutral:

When Aly starred on the Disney show *Phil of the Future*, the costume designer played up her looks with colorful outfits and crazy hairstyles. It added another compelling element to the TV show, but it couldn't have been further from Aly's true style. "My character on the show, Keely, wears a lot of really bright shades, like lime green and orange," she told *Teen People* at the time. "They're fun colors, but I love natural colors." With her long blond hair, nothing looks better than gauzy cream tops and long peasant skirts in dusty browns. That's easy California elegance with just a hint of hippie.

Tip: You don't need to wear shocking colors to get noticed. Try finding shades of cream, camel, or brown that work with your skin tone. It might be a little strange at first if you are used to hot pink and kelly green, but just try it on. Come on, you know you want to. If you are obsessed with drama, wear an entire outfit in the same neutral color. If you walk into the school dance decked out in head-to-toe cream, you'll definitely turn heads.

Don't be a designer snob:

Aly and AJ aren't, so why should you be? Although they have the bank account to buy all those fancy big-name clothes, the sisters say they buy clothes because they like them, not because of the label inside. Sometimes they do don designer duds, but you are just as likely to find them in outfits straight off the rack. Especially when you are young and your style is easy, like AJ and Aly, designer clothes might not be the best fit. They love to troll vintage boutiques for unique duds that are well below department-store prices. "We both love heels, boots, tennis shoes," says AJ. "We love our jeans and we love wearing cool tops and some funky jewelry and we just go for it."

Tip: Don't let the label be the first thing you look at. If you have turned your nose up at secondhand stores in the past, you need an attitude adjustment. There are treasures (at basement prices) to be found! When you walk into school wearing a blouse with a Victorian collar and puff sleeves that looks so punk with your skinny jeans, you don't have to tell anybody you got it from Salvation Army. So get busy bargain hunting.

Be sentimental:

Aly and AJ have matching cross necklaces that they absolutely love. They wear the delicate necklaces, made in the 1800s, whether they are rocking onstage, hanging out at a barbecue, or attending a big party. They are a great reminder of many important things in the sisters' lives.

Tip: *Find your own special style element that brings meaning to your life. Maybe it's friendship bracelets that you and your best friend make for each other and swap to remember a special summer together. Maybe it's a lucky T-shirt you wore when you aced a really hard math test. Only you can decide what has significance. But style doesn't have to be totally superficial.*

Most important: Be your own person!

As Aly and AJ's stylist Paula always counsels the stars she works with, "Be yourself. Be an individual. Have fun, and always dress for you." Aly and AJ have taken Paula's advice to heart. "We've always had our own identity, which is really cool, I think. We're pretty nonconformists," Aly told the *San Antonio Express-News*. AJ's favorite item in her closet is her pair of Frye Boots. These epitomize 1960s cool, but the Frye Company's history is much longer than that. As the oldest continuously operated shoe company in the country, Frye has made boots for soldiers in the American Civil War, the Spanish-American War, Teddy Roosevelt and his Rough Riders, and the pioneers who made their way west to California. That's where hippies and hipsters later fell in love with the bulky toe and chunky heel boot. As for Aly, she prefers more of a surfer vibe and wears her Vans all the time. The slip-on sneakers are comfortable and so supercool with shorts, jeans, or even miniskirts.

Tip: *Wear what you feel comfortable in and what makes you happy. Don't listen to others when making choices for yourself. Enough said!*

CHAPTER THIRTEEN

Discography

When you're a musician, you spend a lot of time listening to other people's music. The process offers insight and inspiration for any artist. Aly and AJ are no exception to this rule. Their taste in music is extremely varied, and their appetite for new bands is voracious. Just like their own performances, the sisters love any music that is heartfelt. But that could describe a lot of different albums. What do the girls really call their favorite?

John Mayer: Well, when Aly and AJ want to be really mellow, they will go into their room, light candles, crack a good book, and put on a John Mayer CD. John is an amazing musician who started out performing acoustic rock but eventually migrated to the blues. All these influences can be heard on his 2006 album *Continuum*, for which he won two Grammy Awards. By then, the Grammys were nothing new to John, who had already received the Song of the Year Award a couple of years earlier for his amazing single "Daughters." John is a cutey, with an amazingly smooth voice. No wonder the girls like to kick back to his tunes.

Sting: The Police, led by front man Sting, is another group always ready in the sisters' CD shuffle. "We grew up listening to them," AJ told the Fort Lauderdale *Sun-Sentinel*. "They're amazing live. They play their own instruments. They're legends, and we really, really appreciate what they've done."

Sting's been around so long, Aly and AJ's parents probably listened to him when they were young. The British singer used to front the new wave band The Police, which released five chart-topping albums between 1978 and 1983. Their sound was unique and mixed punk, reggae, and pop. Hits from The Police like "Every Breath You Take" and "Don't Stand So Close to Me" are still heard on the radio today. After The Police disbanded, Sting went on to a super-successful solo career as well as a hot acting career (sound like anyone else?). He even got his band back. In 2007, he reunited with the other members of The Police, and soon enough they set out on tour. Never say never when it comes to a band getting back together.

Seal: The only thing Seal shares in common with Sting is that they were both born in England (and they have strange names). Even though he studied architecture and engineering in school, Seal's talent as a vocalist couldn't be ignored. His soulful singing has taken many of his songs to the top of the charts in the U.S. and Europe. His sound is super-romantic, especially on his hit "Love's Divine." It sure caught the attention of German supermodel Heidi Klum, whom he married in 2005.

The Fray: Aly and AJ are always on the hunt for new music. One of their latest loves is the band The Fray. The band, which hails from Denver, Colorado, is best known for the song "How to Save a Life," which hit the top three of the *Billboard* Hot 100. That single appeared on both *Scrubs* and *Grey's Anatomy*. No wonder the song sold over 1.2 million copies! Isaac Slade is the lead vocalist and pianist in this four-piece band that continues to rock Aly and AJ's world.

B. B. King: Don't get the wrong idea and think that Aly and AJ are all about Top 40. They love old music just as much as the hottest new singles. They listen to artists that nobody would expect them to, like blues great B. B. King. Known as "the King of Blues," B. B. has truly inspired the sisters. He started strumming out heartbreaking licks on his beloved guitar that he calls Lucille in the 1940s and was still going strong into his eighties!

Jonny Lang: Jonny falls into Aly's and AJ's passion for blues. This Grammy-winning blues guitarist and singer is absolutely gorgeous. Not only that, he released his first album, *Smokin'*, in 1995, when he was only fourteen years old! In fact, Jonny was the first person the sisters ever saw in concert. "We were probably the youngest kids there," AJ recounted to the *Charlotte Observer*. "Jonny Lang is such an amazing musician and singer. He inspired us to pick up the guitar." Well, we're so glad he did!

CHAPTER FOURTEEN

Fun Fast Facts

Aly and AJ have tons of things in common. They love their family, have a deep appreciation for faith, and rock out on their instruments while belting out soulful tunes. That doesn't mean they are exactly the same in every way. For example, AJ is an animal lover and would be a vet if she weren't a big-time rock star. "I love working with . . . dogs or cats, even dolphins," she told *Newsday*. Aly's passion is clothing. "I would be a fashion designer," she said about her plan B. "I even like to cut up clothes now and redesign them. Clothes are kind of my forte." But no matter how different their interests, the sisters are never truly divided because they always come back together to share their experiences.

How do Aly and AJ stack up against each other? Check out the list of fun facts below to see how knowledgeable you are about the Michalka sisters.

fuLL Name:
Amanda Joy
Michalka

AJ's birthdate: APRIL 10, 1991

AJ's zodiac sign: Aries

AJ's height: 5'6"

AJ's favorite COLOR: PURPLE

AJ's favorite book series: His Dark Materials

AJ's favorite TV show: That '70s Show

AJ's favorite actors: Jack Black, Johnny Depp

AJ's favorite actresses: Cameron Diaz

AJ's favorite movie: WiLLOW

AJ's favorite activities: Dancing, cooking, horseback
    riding, mountain biking, and reading

full Name:
Alyson Renae Michalka

ALY's birthDate: March 25, 1989

ALY's zodiac sign: Aries

ALY's height: 5'8"

ALY's favorite colors: black and cranberry

ALY's favorite foods: sushi, pasta, tacos, pop rocks, and ring pops

ALY's favorite school subject: history and language arts

ALY's favorite book series: A series of unfortunate events and Artemis fowl

ALY's favorite activities: hunter-Jumping equestrian, swimming, rock climbing, mountain biking, volleyball, and drawing

ALY's favorite actors: Jack Black, Johnny Depp, and topher Grace

ALY's favorite actresses: Naomi watts and Cate Blanchett

ALY's favorite movies: willow, pirates of the Caribbean, and the school of rock

CHAPTER FIFTEEN:
Web Sightings

If you've read this entire book, you are practically an expert on the lives of Aly and AJ. But these girls are always changing and growing. They love to try new things, whether it's in their personal lives and hobbies or in their musical and acting careers. So you can be sure that this sister sensation will be making news practically every day. To stay on top of the latest information, go to the websites below. But always remember to have an adult around when you go websurfing. That's what Aly and AJ would want!

- Aly and AJ's official site: www.alyandaj.com
- Hollywood Record's website: www.hollywoodrecords. go.com/alyandaj/index.html
- Aly and AJ's MySpace page: www.myspace.com/alyandaj
- A fan site dedicated to Aly and AJ: www.aly-and-aj.com
- Disney's XD: www.disney.go.com/dxd

- Phil of the Future's official website: http://psc.disney.go.com/disneychannel/philofthefuture/index.html

- Aly's IMDB page: www.imdb.com/name/nm1425528/

- AJ's IMDB page: www.imdb.com/name/nm1404488/

- Aly and AJ's Wikipedia page: http://en.wikipedia.org/wiki/Aly_and_AJ